The Pocket Essential

# HITCHHIKER'S GUIDE

First published in Great Britain 2001 by Pocket Essentials, 18 Coleswood Road, Harpenden, Herts, AL5 1EQ

Distributed in the USA by Trafalgar Square Publishing, PO Box 257, Howe Hill Road, North Pomfret, Vermont 05053

Copyright © MJ Simpson 2001
Series Editor: Paul Duncan

A CIP catalogue record for this book is available from the British Library.

ISBN 1-903047-40-4

9 8 7 6 5

Book typeset by Pdunk
Printed and bound by Cox & Wyman

*In memory of Peter Jones (1920-2000)*
*and Douglas Adams (1952-2001)*

## Acknowledgements

In preparing this slim volume, I have been assisted by many people, to whom my thanks are extended: Will Adams, Sophie Astin, Martin Benson, Rayner Bourton, Simon Brett, Jonathan Cecil, Michael Cule, Kevin Davies, Paul Duncan, Jim Francis, Neil Gaiman, Dave Golder, Stephen Grief, Richard Hollis, Roy Hudd, the late Peter Jones, Simon Jones, Lizzy Kremer, Geoffrey McGivern, Dirk Maggs, Joe Melia, Ion Mills, Stephen Moore, Stan Nicholls, Geoffrey Perkins, Andrew Pixley, Terry Platt, Liam Proven, Dave Prowse, Susan Sheridan, Michael Marshall Smith, Aubrey Woods, Matt Zimmerman and - without whom, etc. - Douglas Adams. Apologies if I have missed anyone out.

This book would also not have been possible without the long-term support and encouragement of my parents, without the forbearance and understanding of my wife Hillary, or without the assistance of a small, furry creature from Alpha Centauri.

# CONTENTS

# Foreword by Simon Jones

It's always been a bit of a mystery to me. My old friend Douglas Adams has always maintained that he wrote the character of Arthur Dent, hero/victim of *The Hitchhiker's Guide To The Galaxy*, with me in mind. Personally I've never seen the resemblance. To be brutally frank, he didn't seem anything like me. I mean, Arthur is a man who spends much of his time touring the universe in a dressing gown, in a state of bewilderment bordering on irritability, complaining much of the time about the absence of a really good cup of tea. The irritability stems not just from his state of physical dislocation, but also from a vague sense of unease that nothing is quite what it seems, and never has been. He's easily distracted by trivia, and he keeps thinking it's Thursday.

Actually I think it was a Thursday when I heard from this fellow Mike Simpson. He was in England, and I was in New York, so for me it was a good bit earlier in the morning than it was for him. In fact I'd just got out of bed and put the kettle on.

He came straight to the point. "How would you like to write a foreword to my book about *The Hitchhiker's Guide*?"

Of course, my suspicions were immediately aroused.

"What book? What's it about?"

He replied that it was a complete chronology of all the versions in all media of Douglas' classic work. He added, "You know - all the details of your life as Arthur Dent."

I gave it some thought. Put that way, it sounded really quite interesting, but nonetheless I felt it my duty to wonder aloud, "Is this really something the world needs?"

His reply struck me as a bit sharp in tone. "Yes, it is, or I wouldn't have written it."

"Oh ho!" I thought, "Someone got out of bed the wrong side - and it wasn't me." Actually I can't get out of bed the wrong side, because my wife sleeps on the other - unless I've been on the wrong side all this time and never known it...

I leave him on hold because the kettle has boiled by now, and I have to warm the pot before letting the tea infuse or it'll be undrinkable. As I pour the water on the leaves - while it's boiling, or it's a waste of time - I think about his proposition. He has a point. The world does need this book. I need this book. Once and for all I could prove to people that the radio series came before the books - something a surprising number of people don't know and wilfully won't believe when I tell them. A definitive where-and-when sort of book would settle all sorts of pointless and time-wasting debates. It astonishes me what far-fetched theories are floating out there on the ether. Someone once told me that The Who had planned a rock opera with Roger Daltrey as Arthur and Pete Townsend as The Book - crazy of course, but sort of intriguing. Who was it who came up with the idea that there was a nine-hour experimental German film directed by a disciple of Rainer Werner Fassbinder that's lying forgotten in a deserted cellar in Leipzig? Or did I dream that one?

While I was waiting for the tea to steep, I heard a squawking from the telephone. Mike Simpson was becoming impatient. "Well?" he said, "Will you do it?" He seemed to be in rather a hurry. "Look - I can e-mail you the book if you want to look at it first."

"No, no, don't trouble... or well, maybe, yes, do."

Oh, the Information Superhighway! I've no idea how it works but it still gives me a thrill.

I waited - not very long - and there it was, available to download. Of course that was easier said than done - but after a struggle during which I became convinced that I'd consigned the whole file to oblivion, I had it on screen and, soon after that, printed out. So I read it - and found it very comprehensive, accurate and intriguing. My name's mentioned a lot, and for some reason I find that comforting, I'm not very thrilled to read that I'm too old to play Arthur in the Hollywood movie version. Not enough of a box-office name, I suspect. But if I am too old, it's because I've had to wait so long for it. The eventual cast, if you want my opinion, hasn't even been born yet...

Anyway, I called him back. I congratulated him on his scholarship, and told him I'd be delighted, nay, honoured, to write some sort of foreword - though I wasn't at all sure what I could think of to say. I'd just put down the receiver when I remembered the tea. It had stewed to the colour and consistency of prune juice - a complete waste of prime second flush Assam, which isn't at all easy to come by.

Oh, this book? It's great. Read and enjoy. (Now where have I heard that before?)

Simon Jones
New York, November 2000

# 1: Introduction

Where to begin?

*The Hitchhiker's Guide To The Galaxy* does not follow any sort of pattern. It does not, for example, have any preferred medium. It has been equally successful on radio, on television, on record, as novels, as talking books, on stage or as a computer game. All these different versions tell roughly the same story, but not necessarily in the same way. And on numerous occasions they flatly contradict each other.

This does not make it an easy subject to write a book about. Far from it.

There is no logical sequence to be had here: no season-by-season episode guide, no filmography, not even a clearly defined chronological progression. What there is instead is a genuine multimedia phenomenon - a global success without precedent or parallel. Or, unfortunately, order. I have done my best to make sense of it.

Surprisingly, there has been very little attempt to document this phenomenon (with the obvious exception of Neil Gaiman's out-of-print work, *Don't Panic*) so it is hoped that this book will go some way to explain and chart this incredible story, and the incredible story behind it.

So where to begin?

10.30pm on Wednesday 8th March 1978 is as good a place as any to begin the story of *The Hitchhiker's Guide To The Galaxy*. In those days, the BBC still made a lot of radio comedy, almost invariably written and performed by Oxbridge graduates (the 'alternative comedy' scene was still struggling to find its own identity in a London strip club). Regular listeners to Radio 4 knew to check the *Radio Times* each week, examining certain broadcast slots - 12.27pm, 6.30pm, 10.30pm - for the latest offerings from the Light Entertainment Department at Broadcasting House.

That initial listing for *The Hitchhiker's Guide To The Galaxy* gave no indication that it was to be any different from any of the series before, after, or running concurrently. There was a recognisable name in the cast - Peter Jones, rather mysteriously credited as 'The Book' - and radio comedy obsessives may have recognised writer Douglas Adams' name from a short-lived 1974 Cambridge Footlights spin-off series, *Oh No It Isn't*. The episode title, 'Fit The First', would have seemed a mere whim to most, although fans of Lewis Carroll may have recognised a reference to *The Hunting Of The Snark*. (The Milliways restaurant slogan 'If you've believed six impossible things before breakfast this morning...' was another Carroll reference, although the existence of a 'rule 42' in *Through The Looking Glass* is mere coincidence, according to Adams.) Nevertheless there was no clue as to quite how different this new series was going to be.

For one thing, it did not have an audience. Radio 4 policy was clear: if you were a comedy series, whether sitcom, revue or variety, you had to have an audience. Yet the listeners on that March evening, in their bedsits and their baths, found themselves laughing aloud and alone - which, given the solitary nature of the typical late-night Radio 4 listener, was not as embarrassing as it might have been.

The show was an instant hit, on a scale unseen since the golden age of radio in the 1950s. It very rapidly established itself as worthy of being mentioned in the same breath as radio classics like *Hancock's Half Hour*, *The Goon Show* and *I'm Sorry, I'll Read That Again*.

Real, hard-core, purist *Hitchhiker's Guide* fans still consider the original six-part radio series to be the definitive version of the story. But *The Hitchhiker's Guide To The Galaxy* has a popularity that extends way beyond its hard-core fans, and its numerous incarnations mean that it symbolises different things to different people.

To some it is a cult radio series, to others an early 1980s TV comedy, and to others a series of best-selling science fiction novels. Ironically, Douglas Adams never set out to be either a science fiction writer or a novelist.

If one is to trace the origins of *The Hitchhiker's Guide To The Galaxy*, one has to look at the Footlights Society, that elitist yet prolific group of ever-changing Cambridge undergraduates which has been producing great names in comedy for over a century. The casts of *Monty Python's Flying Circus*, *The Goodies* and *Beyond The Fringe* were wholly or partly composed of Footlights alumni, and the Footlights influence is as strong in *Hitchhiker's Guide* as in any of those other shows. Douglas Adams attended Cambridge University in the early 1970s and there met Simon Jones, Mark Wing-Davey and Geoffrey McGivern, who were to be the inspirations for the characters they were later to play in *The Hitchhiker's Guide To The Galaxy*.

Pinning down just why *The Hitchhiker's Guide To The Galaxy* has been so successful is an impossible task, but there is one very obvious way in which it was truly groundbreaking. It was the first genuinely successful attempt to combine science fiction with comedy. Which is not to say that there had not previously been humorous science fiction, but the works of writers like Harry Harrison or Robert Sheckley were spoofs of the genre, written by and for people familiar with science fiction's conventions and intricacies. They were humorous science fiction, as opposed to science fiction humour.

Attempts at injecting science fiction into more populist comedy were more problematical. American TV producers had managed it briefly with the 1960s sitcom *My Favorite Martian*, but this was simply a strictly Earth-bound fish-out-of-water fantasy along the lines of *I Dream Of Jeannie* or *Bewitched*. The BBC's misguided attempts at this blending of genres resulted in the infamously dire series *Come Back Mrs Noah*, starring Molly Sugden (broadcast after *Hitchhiker's Guide*'s radio debut, but shown as a pilot before it). It was to be another decade before they got it right again with *Red Dwarf*.

Where Douglas Adams succeeded was in writing a story which was actually a satire on human existence and foibles, just blown up to a galactic scale. In that respect his predecessors were people like Jonathan Swift whose *Gulliver's Travels* ploughed a similar furrow. Adams has always maintained that he didn't set out to write a science fiction series, but after blowing up the world in the first episode, he was left with no other choice.

One of the reasons for the series' initial success was undoubtedly the science fiction fever which gripped the UK, and indeed the world, in the late 1970s, fuelled by the massive success of *Star Wars*. George Lucas' film, which had created a media craving for anything to do with spaceships, aliens or robots, very fortuitously opened across the UK in January 1978, less than six weeks before *Hitchhiker's Guide* debuted. However, the BBC commissioned Douglas Adams to write 'Fit The First' in March 1977, before *Star Wars* even opened in America, and certainly before the SF hype began.

Despite his best efforts to deny the label, Douglas Adams is now irrevocably branded as a science fiction author, and a spectacularly successful one at that, whose books can command enormous advances. He is also an almost evangelical advocate of new technology, from his early experiments with computers that produced, for example, the distorted self-portrait on the cover of *The Hitchhiker's Guide To The Galaxy: The Original Radio Scripts*, to his current directorship of h2g2 (formerly The Digital Village) and his position as one of the most sought-after speakers for technology conferences.

Above all this, above and beyond the success of *The Hitchhiker's Guide To The Galaxy*, the state-of-the-art Apple Macintoshes, the world's largest collection of left-handed guitars and the endless globe-trotting, one thing asserts itself time and again as one reads this book and follows the story of Douglas Adams' success.

He has – how should one phrase this? – never quite got the hang of deadlines.

Everybody who has ever worked with Douglas Adams has encountered this problem, and tales are legion of the author being locked in hotel rooms to finish novels or scribbling last-minute changes to scripts on toilet paper. Not all of these stories are apocryphal. Even more incredibly, this inability to meet deadlines seems to be transferable and has affected even aspects of the *Hitchhiker's Guide* canon with which Adams himself was not directly involved. Publicists around the globe throw their hands up in horror when presented with a new Douglas Adams project because there is no way of knowing when, if ever, it will appear. *The Salmon Of Doubt*, for example, a novel which may involve Dirk Gently, may be *Hitchhiker's Guide* volume 6 or may be something completely different, has now been, 'in the works,' for over five years. As for the much-vaunted feature film version of *The Hitchhiker's Guide To The Galaxy*... well, see the relevant chapter for details of how long we have all been waiting for that.

Fortunately, Douglas Adams is actually not very prolific. As an author, he has published only seven novels in 21 years, of which two were largely derived from radio scripts, and two were based on *Doctor Who* stories. Never afraid to reformat material into new media, Adams has something of a reputation for recycling - for an example of what his friends think of this, see the spot-on spoof that was included in the 1986 Mel Smith/Griff Rhys Jones paperback, *The Lavishly Tooled Smith And Jones Instant Coffee Table Book* (or listen to almost any episode of *The Burkiss Way*).

Many ideas from *Hitchhiker's Guide* have become common cultural currency in the past two decades, notably phrases such as 'life, don't talk to me about life,' and, 'large, friendly letters,' but the most celebrated element of the entire *Hitchhiker's Guide* saga is the idea that there is a single, definitive answer to all the questions of the universe, and that it is the number 42. More than any other aspect of the story, the significance of 42 and the phrase which pre-empted it, 'life, the universe and everything,' have become enshrined in the cultural Zeitgeist of the late 20th century (and now the 21st).

Scientists have for many years been searching for a single, unifying theory of everything, and consequently *Hitchhiker's Guide* and its central joke has always been enormously popular among the scientific community. Even Arthur C Clarke referred to 42 as the meaning of life in his novel *Rama Revealed*. In fact, the idea that a single number may lie at the heart of all science is not inconceivable, given the range of factors which have a constant numerical value. Pi, e, c and the Avogadro constant are just four examples of numerical absolutes liable to be encountered by students of maths or physics, although none of them admittedly are a nice, round integer like 42.

Adams has stated that he picked 42 because it was, "the most humorous of the two-figure numbers," and is undoubtedly fed up with questions from fans, some of whom seem to think that the number has genuine (probably hilarious) significance but just needs to be explained a wee bit more. An audible groan can be heard at Adams' talks whenever someone asks him why he chose 42, presumably believing that (a) he has not been asked this before, or (b) his previous explanations have somehow passed the questioner by.

There are many coincidental appearances of 42 in literature, the media and the world, some of which (if created after 1978) may be deliberate homages to *Hitchhiker's Guide*. However most occurrences of the number are merely coincidental, and not particularly interesting coincidences at that. In any corner shop or supermarket there will be items which cost 42p, in any reasonably sized street there will be a house number 42. Every individual encounters scores of two-figure numbers every day, and on a purely statistical level, approximately one per cent of those are likely to be 42. (In fact, since smaller numbers are more common - they occur in both small groups and large groups - and 42 lies in the bottom half of the range 1-99, it will likely account for slightly more than one per cent.)

There is no special significance to 42. That, in fact, is precisely what makes the joke so funny.

Clear proof of 42's ordinariness lies in the fact that other two-figure numbers have just as much significance to other groups of fans. Readers of Robert Anton Wilson and Robert Shea's *Illuminatus* trilogy, for example, know the importance of 23 and how frequently it occurs, while fans of American musical japester 'Weird Al' Yankovic watch out for occurrences of 27 and find them just as often. It is obvious that Douglas Adams could have picked any reasonably sized number for Deep Thought's answer and it would have been discovered to crop up elsewhere on a frequent basis. The one and only significance to 42 is that (in English, at least) it sounds amusing with its 'or,' 'ee' and 'oo' sounds. That's it. That is the sum total significance of 42. It's a funny-sounding word.

None of which is likely to prevent somebody from standing up at Douglas Adams' next public Q&A session and asking, with a look-at-me grin on their face, why he chose that particular number.

The storyline of *The Hitchhiker's Guide To The Galaxy* is complex, contradictory and unfailingly bizarre, full of inexplicable events and weird characters. The story behind *The Hitchhiker's Guide To The Galaxy* is just as complex, contradictory and bizarre, and is equally full of inexplicable events and weird characters. The one perfectly complements the other.

This book is an attempt to sort the story of the past 23 years into something approaching order. To research this book, I have ploughed through two decades' worth of the fanzine *Mostly Harmless* (published by the Official *Hitchhiker's Guide To The Galaxy* Appreciation Society, ZZ9 Plural Z Alpha, and still the only source on the planet for regular *Hitchhiker's Guide* news and features). I have also read dozens of articles and interviews in magazines and on the web, and I have delved into my own personal archives of *Hitchhiker's Guide* ephemera and original interviews.

I have done everything I can, but there is one factor beyond my control. This book is due for publication in April 2001, but if it's late - well, that's the fault of the subject matter, not the author!

Where then, should we actually begin?

Why not begin in a field outside Innsbruck in 1971, where 19-year-old Douglas Adams is lying drunk under a starry sky? Gazing at his well-thumbed copy of the essential undergraduate travel book, *The Hitchhiker's Guide To Europe*, he wonders whether somebody could write a similar volume for interstellar travellers - *The Hitchhiker's Guide To The Galaxy*.

That was thirty years ago...

MJ Simpson
Leicester, October 2000

## *Introduction To The Second Edition*

Douglas Adams passed away suddenly in May 2001, shortly after the publication of this book's first edition. For this second edition, Chapter 13 has been revised and updated, and an Afterword has been added to bring the story up to date. A few minor typographical errors have also been corrected.

MJ Simpson
Leicester, August 2001

Note: The title *The Hitchhiker's Guide To The Galaxy* has enjoyed numerous different 'official' spellings over the years, with various hyphens, apostrophes, spaces, etc. The version used in this book – with 'Hitchhiker' as a single, unhyphenated word, is Douglas Adams' prefered spelling and is used herein for all versions of the story, irrespective of the actual spelling on the relevant book jacket, record sleeve, title sequence, etc

Feedback on this book is positively encouraged, and may be sent c/o Pocket Essentials, or directly to mjsimpson@btinternet.com

# 2: The Radio Series

## *The Primary Phase*

### Fit The First

First broadcast: 8th March 1978

Cast: Peter Jones, Simon Jones, Geoffrey McGivern, Bill Wallis, Jo Kendall, David Gooderson

*Story*: Arthur Dent wakes up one morning to discover that his house is about to be knocked down to make way for a bypass. Before this can happen, he discovers that his friend Ford Prefect is an alien and that, furthermore, Earth is about to be demolished to make way for a hyperspace bypass.

Ford turns out to be a travelling researcher for an electronic guidebook, *The Hitchhiker's Guide To The Galaxy*, and successfully transports himself and Arthur onto the Vogon Constructor ship moments before it destroys the planet. Arthur is given a Babel fish in his ear to help him understand alien languages and a towel for everything else. Unfortunately, the Vogons have detected their arrival on the ship and the Vogon captain, Prostetnic Vogon Jeltz, tortures them with some of his poetry, Vogon poetry being the third worst in the universe.

### Fit The Second

First broadcast: 15th March 1978

Cast: Peter Jones, Simon Jones, Geoffrey McGivern, Bill Wallis, David Tate, Susan Sheridan, Mark Wing-Davey, Stephen Moore

*Story*: After unsuccessfully attempting to flatter the Vogon Captain, Arthur and Ford are thrown off the ship but are unexpectedly picked up by the *Heart Of Gold*, a spaceship powered by the Infinite Improbability Drive. Improbable as it may seem, the stolen spaceship is under the command of Zaphod Beeblebrox, part-time Galactic President and a distant relative of Ford's, accompanied by his human girlfriend, Tricia 'Trillian' McMillan. Zaphod met Trillian at a party in Islington where she was being chatted up by Arthur.

The ship is also equipped with two products of the Sirius Cybernetics Corporation's 'Genuine People Personalities' programme: an overly cheerful computer named Eddie and a manically depressed robot called Marvin.

## Fit The Third

First broadcast: 22nd March 1978

Cast: Peter Jones, Simon Jones, Geoffrey McGivern, David Tate, Susan Sheridan, Mark Wing-Davey, Stephen Moore, Richard Vernon

*Story*: The *Heart Of Gold* moves into orbit around the legendary planet Magrathea, once the home of a custom planet-building industry. Two automated guided missiles aimed at the ship are rendered harmless when Arthur switches on the Infinite Improbability Drive and they turn into a bowl of petunias and a sperm whale. In the chaos, Trillian's two pet mice escape.

Landing on the planet, Zaphod, Trillian and Ford explore the underground remains of the Magrathean civilisation, leaving Arthur and Marvin on the planet's surface. Arthur bumps into a Magrathean named Slartibartfast who takes him into the planet and shows him the Earth Mk.2...

## Fit The Fourth

First broadcast: 29th March 1978

Cast: Peter Jones, Simon Jones, Geoffrey McGivern, Susan Sheridan, Mark Wing-Davey, Richard Vernon, Jim Broadbent, Jonathan Adams, Ray Hassett, Jeremy Browne, Peter Hawkins, David Tate

*Story*: Slartibartfast explains to Arthur that the Earth was originally built by Magrathea as a commission for the pan-dimensional beings known as mice, but was destroyed five minutes before its task was completed. Arthur watches recordings that show how the pan-dimensional beings originally built an enormous computer to calculate the answer to the great question of life, the universe and everything. The computer was called Deep Thought, and after seven and a half million years it announced that the answer was 42.

So a bigger computer, called the Earth, was built to find out what the actual question was, but five minutes before the final read-out, the Vogons blew it up.

Arthur meets up again with Ford, Zaphod and Trillian who are being entertained by Trillian's white mice, Frankie and Benjy. The mice hope that Arthur can help them find the question, but the meeting is interrupted when sirens announce the arrival of galactic cops, chasing the stolen *Heart Of Gold*. The four fugitives hide behind a computer bank which then explodes.

# Fit The Fifth

First broadcast: 5th April 1978

Cast: Peter Jones, Simon Jones, Geoffrey McGivern, Susan Sheridan, Mark Wing-Davey, Stephen Moore, Anthony Sharp, Roy Hudd

*Story*: Recovering from the effects of the exploding computer, Arthur, Ford, Zaphod and Trillian find themselves in Milliways, 'The Restaurant At The End Of The Universe.' This is a swish eatery built on the ruins of Magrathea at a point in the space-time continuum just before the heat-death of the universe. They find that Marvin has been on the planet all this time and now works as a Milliways car park attendant.

Zaphod and Ford take a liking to an extremely black spaceship in the car park and steal it with Marvin's help. However, the ship is outside their control and dumps them into the middle of an intergalactic war.

# Fit The Sixth

First broadcast: 12th April 1978

Cast: Peter Jones, Simon Jones, Geoffrey McGivern, Susan Sheridan, Mark Wing-Davey, Stephen Moore, Aubrey Woods, Jonathan Cecil, David Jason, Beth Porter

*Story*: Arthur and Co. are dismayed to realise that they have stolen the Haggunenon Admiral's flagship. They are mystified by two video communications from a Haggunenon officer who not only thinks that Zaphod and Trillian are both the Admiral, but appears in two completely different shapes.

It transpires that Haggunenons are super-evolutionary life forms who constantly change shape - and the real Admiral is in fact the chair they have been sitting in! He evolves into a copy of the Ravenous Bugblatter Beast of Traal and eats Zaphod, Trillian and Marvin, but Ford and Arthur escape in an emergency escape capsule.

The capsule dumps them inside a massive 'ark in space' containing the useless third of the population of the planet Golgafrincham. Commanded by a Captain in a bath, this non-steerable spaceship crash-lands on a primitive planet which they name Fintlewoodlewix but which Ford and Arthur recognise as prehistoric Earth. The arrival of the Golgafrinchan hairdressers and telephone sanitisers has, unknown to anyone, completely upset the Earth's programming - so it will never produce the right question even if the Vogons don't blow it up. Resigned to their fate, Arthur and Ford wander off to explore the planet.

*Background*: In February 1977, writer Douglas Adams met with producer Simon Brett to discuss a science fiction comedy series called *The Ends Of The Earth*. It was to be an anthology show, in which the world was destroyed in a different way each week. In the first episode, the world was destroyed to make way for a hyperspace bypass. Somehow, that story mutated into *The Hitchhiker's Guide To The Galaxy*.

A pilot script was commissioned in March, written in April and recorded in June.

It wasn't, of course, that simple. Cambridge graduate Adams had grown up in an era of overblown rock concept albums and wanted his radio series to have similar production values. Not just isolated sound effects but ridiculously huge soundscapes, integrating dialogue, music and wildly imaginative sounds into a holistic presentation.

He also wanted a narrator, but not a studio audience. The BBC were adamant that radio comedy had to have an audience or the listeners would not know when to laugh. That Simon Brett successfully lobbied for *Hitchhiker's Guide* to be an exception was fortunate not just for Douglas Adams, but for radio audiences generally. Those at home would have had the programme's atmosphere ruined by howls of laughter, while those in the studio would have had to stay there for days and still not have understood the programme unless they also successfully blagged their way into the editing suite.

As for the narrator: every book on radio writing will tell you to avoid this device. It never works. Except (point out the more recent volumes) in the case of *The Hitchhiker's Guide To The Galaxy*. What Adams did was to cleverly integrate his narrator into the story as the audio read-out of his intergalactic travel book.

At this point, Adams was 25 and had been scraping a living since graduation with a succession of bizarre jobs, including being a bodyguard for an Arabian royal family. All the while, he had been trying to make a go of it as a scriptwriter, but even collaboration with an established name like Graham Chapman had not brought him success, and he had only a handful of incredibly obscure radio and TV credits to his name. All this was about to change.

The first task was to cast the series, and for this Adams turned to his old friends from the Cambridge Footlights Society. The characters of Arthur Dent, Ford Prefect and Zaphod Beeblebrox were based to some extent on actors Simon Jones, Geoffrey McGivern and Mark Wing-Davey, and the BBC was still sufficiently an old boy network for this casting to be passed (actually, Wing-Davey as Zaphod did not appear until 'Fit The Second.')

The biggest problem was the narrator. Adams wanted a 'Peter Jones'-y type of voice, a crisp, English, rather old-world, slightly confused but terribly certain sort of voice. After approaching Michael Palin and one or two other people, it was suggested that possibly Peter Jones had a suitably 'Peter Jones'-y voice, and the actor was approached. Jones was a veteran of radio comedy, not just from his work on *Just A Minute*, but also from *In All Directions*, a very popular 1960s show written by Frank Muir and Denis Norden, in which Jones starred with Peter Ustinov.

The pilot show was recorded in June 1977, with the actors gazing out over the unusually empty stalls of the Paris Studio, London. Two months later, the go-ahead for five more episodes was given. However, by this point Simon Brett was working in television, so the producer's chair was handed over to Geoffrey Perkins (now BBC Head of Comedy).

At this point, the storyline proper began to take shape, although as Perkins recalls, "Douglas was writing it episode by episode, without any clear idea where he was going, but it meant that if something was good, we could bring it back. Marvin, for example, I said we should keep, but Douglas thought he had used up the idea. I said 'No, look. The whole world of this series keeps changing all the time. We've got to keep some core characters.'"

Episodes 2-4 were recorded in November and December 1977, but the final two parts were postponed until February 1978, perilously close to the broadcast date. This was because, after years of relative failure, Adams suddenly found himself writing not only *Hitchhiker's Guide* but also a four-part *Doctor Who* adventure, 'The Pirate Planet' (see Chapter 11). Television schedules being far more immutable than radio ones, *Doctor Who* took precedence over *Hitchhiker's Guide*, and when that script was complete, Adams was simply too exhausted to finish the remaining two *Hitchhiker's Guide* episodes.

Enter John Lloyd, a man who subsequently proved to be one of the most important names in British television comedy, helping to create *Not The Nine O'Clock News*, *Spitting Image*, *Blackadder* and the TV version of *Hitchhiker's Guide*. In 1978 he was working for BBC Radio as producer of *Week Ending*.

Lloyd had known Adams since the days of Footlights and was working on his own science fiction comedy, provisionally entitled *GiGax*, which he subsequently described as something he was, "ineffectually tinkering with in the year or two before *Hitchhiker's* swam into Douglas' ken." With Adams needing good, funny, science fiction ideas quick, Lloyd agreed to collaborate on the remaining episodes of *Hitchhiker's Guide*, plundering ideas from his *GiGax* notes. Among his contributions were The Book's speech on the Triganic Pu and other intergalactic currency, and the Haggunenons with their super-evolutionary skills.

The final episode of the first series of *Hitchhiker's Guide* was recorded just eight days before 'Fit The First' was scheduled for broadcast, setting a dangerous precedent in terms of deadlines. The series went out with only a brief paragraph to publicise it in *Radio Times* and was favourably reviewed in two Sunday newspapers. Simon Brett recalled: "When the first one went out, I saw Douglas later that week and he said 'Have there been any press reviews?' And I said to him, rather patronisingly, 'Oh Douglas, come on. This is a radio programme. You know how much coverage radio gets.' But he was absolutely right."

By the end of its first run, *Hitchhiker's Guide* had attracted a significant audience, although the BBC remained unsure of what to do with the show. According to Geoffrey Perkins, "Halfway through the first run we got an audience figure in and it was 0.0, which meant that theoretically, no one was listening to it. But I was getting 20-30 letters a day, maybe more. We really knew it was a hit when we got a letter which had just been addressed to, 'Megadodo Publications, Megadodo House, Ursa Minor,' and somebody had written in the corner, 'Try BBC.' I thought if the Post Office had heard of us, we must have made it."

Enquiring about further exploitation of the series, Douglas Adams received a letter from BBC Enterprises which said, "In our experience, books and records of radio series don't sell," a bad move which may reasonably be compared with Decca turning down the Beatles or Universal passing on the chance to make *Star Wars*. Instead, the novelisation rights went to Pan and the album rights to Original Records.

*Comment*: Although 'Fit The First' offered few clues about where *The Hitchhiker's Guide To The Galaxy* would lead to - over the next five weeks or the following 23 years - it nevertheless stood out among contemporary radio comedy as something special.

In retrospect, the script seems a little formulaic and its Footlights roots show, nowhere more clearly than in the character of Lady Cynthia Fitzmelton. This 'Penelope Keith/Margaret Thatcher type' (played by Jo Kendall of *I'm Sorry I'll Read That Again* and *The Burkiss Way*) has a self-contained monologue in which she officially 'launches' the demolition of Arthur Dent's house, making a small speech before breaking a bottle of champagne on a bulldozer. Dropped from all subsequent versions, Lady Cynthia could have appeared in any Footlights smoking concert of the 1970s without seeming out of place.

There are many other unique aspects to this version which sound strange to those more familiar with the subsequent books and TV series. For example, it seems odd that Arthur, not Ford, should persuade Mr Prosser to lie down in the mud. (As Geoffrey Perkins once commented: "Douglas always had a problem about 'What is a character?' - he tended to swap dialogue between characters at will.") But it is in episodes 5 and 6 that the radio series shows its uniqueness with the Haggunenon storyline. In all subsequent versions (except a few stage productions), the ship which the main characters steal belongs to the rock group Disaster Area and the Haggunenons have been largely forgotten.

Nevertheless, nearly a quarter century later, the original six-episode radio series of *The Hitchhiker's Guide To The Galaxy* remains an extremely funny and absolutely groundbreaking slice of British radio comedy, as well as a defining moment in the development of science fiction humour.

## *The Secondary Phase*

### Fit The Seventh

First broadcast: 24th December 1978
Cast: Peter Jones, Simon Jones, Geoffrey McGivern, Mark Wing-Davey, Stephen Moore, Bill Paterson, David Tate, Alan Ford
*Story*: An Arcturan Megafreighter approaching Ursa Minor Beta, home of the *Hitchhiker's Guide To The Galaxy* offices, finds it has an unusual stowaway: Zaphod Beeblebrox. Zaphod escaped from the Haggunenon when it evolved into an escape pod, and then received a message implanted in his brain (by himself) telling him to find a man called Zarniwoop.

Meanwhile, Arthur and Ford are still stuck on prehistoric Fintlewoodlewix and are happily drunk when they spot a spaceship fading in and out of reality.

In the lobby of the *Hitchhiker's Guide* offices, Zaphod bumps into Marvin and the two of them head up in the lift to Zarniwoop's office. But the building is attacked by Frogstar fighters looking for Zaphod. Marvin tricks a giant Frogstar robot into destroying itself while Zaphod makes his escape with a strange man named Roosta. But the Frogstar fighters simply steal the whole building, with Zaphod and Roosta inside.

### Fit The Eighth

First broadcast: 21st January 1980
Cast: Peter Jones, Simon Jones, Geoffrey McGivern, Mark Wing-Davey, Stephen Moore, David Tate, Alan Ford, Valentine Dyall
*Story*: Zaphod and Roosta are taken to the Frogstar, home of the ultimate psychic torture device, the Total Perspective Vortex, and its guardian, Gargravarr. Meanwhile, Ford and Arthur realise that the spaceship they can see will only solidify in their reality if they stop drinking. They do so and the

spaceship - the *Heart Of Gold* - lands, very heavily and badly. From it staggers Zaphod.

It seems that Ford had somehow lost his towel, which became fossilised, then encased in a meteor derived from the explosion of the Earth. Zaphod found the meteor, spotted the towel and came back in time to rescue them.

Zaphod explains how he escaped from the Total Perspective Vortex. The device is designed to make the victim see how totally insignificant they are in universal terms; Zaphod survived the experience because it showed him that he actually *was* the most important being in the universe, as he suspected!

## Fit The Ninth

First broadcast: 22nd January 1980

Cast: Peter Jones, Simon Jones, Geoffrey McGivern, Mark Wing-Davey, Stephen Moore, Bill Wallis, David Tate, Loueen Willoughby, Richard Goolden

*Story*: The *Heart Of Gold* finds itself pursued by a Vogon fleet, commanded by Prostetnic Vogon Jeltz, who is apparently in league with Zaphod's personal analyst, Gag Halfrunt. Arthur finds a Nutrimatic Drinks Dispenser on board and tries to explain to it how to make a cup of tea.

When the Vogons attack, the *Heart Of Gold* cannot escape because all its computer circuits have been diverted to working out why Arthur wants tea. Zaphod holds a seance to contact his great-grandfather, who turns out to be aware of the mission to find Zarniwoop and helpfully solves the tea problem - Arthur wants tea because he's an ignorant monkey who doesn't know any better - thus allowing the ship to escape.

## Fit The Tenth

First broadcast: 23rd January 1980

Cast: Peter Jones, Simon Jones, Geoffrey McGivern, Mark Wing-Davey, Stephen Moore, David Tate, Rula Lenska, Ronald Baddiley, John Baddeley, John le Mesurier

*Story*: The *Heart Of Gold* materialises in a strange, smooth cave, high up on the planet Brontitall. Arthur and Marvin fall out of the cave, and Zaphod and Ford nearly follow them.

Arthur lands on the back of a giant bird who shows him that the 'cave' is in fact part of a fifteen-mile-high statue called 'Arthur Dent Throwing The Nutrimatic Cup.' Arthur is taken to a bird colony in the statue's ear where the leader of the bird people explains how the planet Brontitall became infested with friendly robots. Then one night a vision appeared of Arthur

22

arguing with the Nutrimatic Drinks Dispenser and the people of Brontitall realised that they did not have to be friendly back to the robots, so they banished them from the planet and built the statue in Arthur's honour. They later evolved into birds because of a second plague which they are reluctant to discuss.

Ford and Zaphod finally fall out of the cup, also landing on a bird. Meanwhile Arthur Dent travels down to the planet's surface, where he is attacked by a foot warrior from the Dolmansaxlil Shoe Corporation but rescued by an attractive archaeologist named Lintilla.

## Fit The Eleventh

First broadcast: 24th January 1980

Cast: Peter Jones, Simon Jones, Geoffrey McGivern, Mark Wing-Davey, Stephen Moore, David Tate, Rula Lenska, John Baddeley, Mark Smith

*Story*: As Ford and Zaphod escape from a flock of angry birds, Lintilla introduces Arthur to Lintilla and Lintilla, explaining that due to an accident there are 578,000,000,000 Lintilla clones in the universe. The other Lintillas are delighted that their archaeological dig has suddenly been helped by the unexplained opening-up of a deep shaft (caused, unknown to them, by Marvin's fifteen-mile plummet from the cup).

A layer of crushed shoes explains the planet's second plague. It passed the Shoe Event Horizon, the point at which only shoe shops are built and the economy collapses. Arthur and the Lintillas are captured by Higg Hurtenflurst, a Dolmansaxlil executive who shows them why shoes are important, but they are rescued by Marvin.

Meanwhile, Ford and Zaphod escape the birds by hiding in a derelict spaceport where, incredibly, one spaceship seems to be still functioning.

## Fit The Twelfth

First broadcast: 25th January 1980

Cast: Peter Jones, Simon Jones, Geoffrey McGivern, Mark Wing-Davey, Stephen Moore, David Tate, Rula Lenska, Ken Campbell, Jonathan Pryce

*Story*: Escaping from the Dolmansaxlil headquarters, Arthur, Marvin and the three Lintillas encounter a strange man named Poodoo who is accompanied by a priest and three male anticlones all called Allitnil. The Lintillas and Allitnils instantly fall in love and Poodoo's priest sets about marrying them. As the first Allitnil kisses his bride, they both disappear, and the second couple follow straight afterwards.

As Zaphod and Ford explore the spaceship they have found, the passengers all suddenly wake up and start panicking. Zaphod and Ford seek refuge in the cockpit where they meet... Zarniwoop!

Cutting back to Arthur's story, we find that he has killed the third Allitnil, so he, Marvin and the remaining Lintilla make their escape and head off to a nearby abandoned spaceport. Zarniwoop explains to Ford and Zaphod that they have been in an artificial universe all along. It was all a plan to bring Zarniwoop the *Heart Of Gold*, the only ship capable of taking him to the home of the ruler of the universe.

On an otherwise uninhabited planet, a man lives in a shack with his pet cat. Zarniwoop, Zaphod, Arthur and Ford visit him - for he is the ruler of the universe. The reason that the Man in the Shack is capable of ruling is that he believes only what he can see and hear himself, so he does not believe that the rest of the universe exists and can make completely objective decisions.

The man lets slip that Zaphod was behind the analysts' and Vogons' plan to destroy the Earth and Arthur, in a huff, returns to the *Heart Of Gold*. As the ship blasts off with Arthur, Lintilla and Marvin on board, Zaphod, Ford and Zarniwoop are left stranded on the planet...

*Background*: Although generally considered part of series two (or 'The Secondary Phase' as it became known much later), 'Fit The Seventh' was written and recorded entirely separately. It was recorded in November 1978 and broadcast over Christmas, more than a year before 'Fit The Eighth.' To all intents and purposes, this was *The Hitchhiker's Guide To The Galaxy Christmas Special* - however, as Douglas Adams subsequently pointed out: "It had nothing to do with Christmas and was not aired on Christmas Day. Those are the only two known connections with Christmas."

The original plan had been to base the story around the Nativity, with the star that guides the Wise Men actually being the hapless Marvin plummeting through the atmosphere and smashing into a Bethlehem stable. Given the controversy which surrounded the release of *Monty Python's Life Of Brian* the following year, the decision to abandon this storyline was remarkably prudent. By this point, the first series had already been repeated twice, and Douglas Adams was busy writing the novelisation.

The second series hit problems almost straight away. 'Fit The Eighth' took three days to record in May 1979, and 'Fit The Ninth' was postponed the following month. Part of the problem was that Adams was still desperately trying to finish his novel.

In May, *Hitchhiker's Guide* was adapted as a stage play; in July it was re-recorded as an LP; in August it was nominated for a Hugo (the highest award in science fiction) at the World Science Fiction Convention.

In September, David Hatch (Controller, BBC Radio 4), told Geoffrey Perkins that he would like to broadcast the second series of *Hitchhiker's Guide* in a single week in January. 'Fit The Ninth' was finally committed to tape in November; one of the episode's highlights was a choir of robots singing the Sirius Cybernetics Corporation company song, 'Share And Enjoy', the making of which was filmed and shown on television as part of a schools programme. 'Fit The Tenth' followed in December, by which time Adams was already working on a pilot script for a TV version. The final two episodes were recorded in January, just in time for broadcast. 'Fit The Twelfth' was in fact still being mixed less than an hour before it was due to air, and was subsequently remixed for repeats.

The *Radio Times* for that week gave *Hitchhiker's Guide* the front cover and a big feature inside. However, as it went to press before the final episode was recorded, the character of the Man in the Shack was still uncast and was credited to the anagrammatical Ron Hate (it was actually Stephen Moore).

*Comment*: The second radio series is one of the forgotten gems of the *Hitchhiker's Guide* canon. Although a few of the ideas were incorporated into the second novel, knowledge of this storyline is evidence of a real *Hitchhiker's Guide* fan.

There are some fantastic ideas here, possibly too many: the Total Perspective Vortex, the Shoe Event Horizon, the plague of robots, the statue of 'Arthur Dent Throwing The Nutrimatic Cup' (with its giant floating cup held in position by art), the Lintilla clones and finally the ruler of the Universe.

Because of the limits of the six-part series (or strictly speaking, a special and a five-part series), and especially because of the desperate race to record the final three episodes, much of the script seems rushed and no sooner are we introduced to one plot point than we have to move onto another. Nevertheless, true fans of *Hitchhiker's Guide* rate the second radio series very highly.

In 1985, all twelve radio scripts were published as *The Hitchhiker's Guide To The Galaxy: The Original Radio Scripts*, including copious amounts of unheard material and extensive footnotes by both Douglas Adams and Geoffrey Perkins.

## The Tertiary Phase

There was very nearly a third radio series of *The Hitchhiker's Guide To The Galaxy*. It was suggested in 1993 by BBC Enterprises when they noticed how well the tapes and CDs of the original series were selling.

After Neil Gaiman turned down the job, a successful radio writer named Alick Rowe was set the task of adapting *Life, The Universe And Everything* into an eight-part radio series. An experienced producer named Dirk Maggs was appointed to oversee the project, scheduled to be recorded in October that year and broadcast in November. The original cast were contacted, and Brian Johnstone and Fred Truman agreed to play the cricket commentators in the first episode. Unfortunately, Rowe's first draft was deemed unsuitable and the project was rescheduled for the following June. In April 1994 'The Tertiary Phase' was announced as being on hold, and the last that was ever heard of it was in July 1994 when it was said to be still, "under discussion."

*Life, The Universe And Everything* has in fact been successfully adapted for the radio twice. Unfortunately one version is in German and one is in Finnish!

The final radio appearance of *The Hitchhiker's Guide To The Galaxy* was a half-hour documentary in 1998 to mark the series' twentieth anniversary. Peter Jones provided *Hitchhiker's Guide*-style narration for the programme, which was called *The Guide To Twenty Years' Hitchhiking* and later released on cassette as *Douglas Adams' Guide To The Hitchhiker's Guide To The Galaxy*.

# 3: The Stage Productions

It may surprise many people to discover that the first ever adaptation of *The Hitchhiker's Guide To The Galaxy* - before it was a book, a TV series, an LP or even a second radio series - was a stage play. For more than 20 years, *Hitchhiker's Guide* has been a popular, if intermittent, title in the theatrical world. It has been performed on three continents, by a wide variety of professional and amateur casts. However, it is the first three productions which are of most note.

## *The Science Fiction Theatre Of Liverpool Production*

Dates: May 1979
Venue: Institute for Contemporary Arts, London
Director: Ken Campbell
Cast: Chris Langham, Richard Hope, Mitch Davies, Stephen Williams, Sue Jones-Davies, Russell Denton, Cindy Oswin, Maya Sendalle, Roger Sloman, John Joyce, Neil Cunningham.

Ken Campbell is a legend of British theatre, and his Science Fiction Theatre of Liverpool was responsible for such memorable productions as *Illuminatus!*, *The Warp* (the longest play ever performed), and *The Hitchhiker's Guide To The Galaxy*, which he adapted himself from the first series' radio scripts.

Realising that an offbeat, original story like *Hitchhiker's Guide* required an offbeat, original presentation, Campbell hit on the inspired notion of reversing the traditional physical structure of a theatre. Rather than have the audience sit passively while the actors strode on and off stage, he devised a way for the actors to remain stationary while the audience moved around.

To this end, a seating platform was built which worked on a hovercraft principle. Balancing on a cushion of air a fraction of a millimetre above the floor of the ICA auditorium, it could be pushed around by stagehands, thus pointing the audience towards whichever of the actors (scattered around the walls on platforms of various heights) was talking.

Of course, this technique severely limited the size of the audience, with only 80 seats available for each of the nine performances. The show sold out in a flash and there was simply no way that any extra seats could be found - even for the radio cast. As Simon Jones recalls, "When I said I was Arthur Dent they looked at me as though I'd said I was the Queen of Sheba."

The problem of Zaphod's second head was solved by having two actors strapped together in one costume, while The Book's narration was, in a never-repeated touch, shared between two usherettes, named Lithos and Terros. The play actually began in the foyer of the ICA, with the two usherettes inviting the audience into the auditorium to escape the imminent destruction of the Earth. Cindy Oswin, who played Lithos, shortly afterwards played Trillian on the *Hitchhiker's Guide* LPs. Campbell himself would play Poodoo in the final episode of the second radio series.

Arthur was played by Chris Langham who was only available because the first series of *Not The Nine O'Clock News*, in which he was a regular, had been postponed until after the general election. He was also one of the writers on *The Muppet Show* and later wrote and starred in the sitcom *Kiss Me Kate*. Also notable among the cast are Sue Jones-Davies (Judith in *Life Of Brian* as Trillian); John Joyce, who later presented a one-man show based on the work of Philip K Dick; and Roger Sloman, best-known for Mike Leigh's *Nuts In May*.

In direct contrast to the success of the small-scale ICA production, the second (and last) London production of *The Hitchhiker's Guide To The Galaxy* would prove to be an unmitigated disaster.

## *The Rainbow Theatre Production*

Dates: July-August 1980
Venue: Rainbow Theatre, London
Director: Ken Campbell
Cast: Roger Blake, Kim Durham, David Brett, John Terence, Nicholas d'Avirro, Jude Alderson, David Learner, Mike Cule, Lewis Cowen, James Castle, David Atkinson, Beverly Andrews, Doretta Dunkley, Kenteas Brine

Though it has been a success in many media in many countries, *Hitchhiker's Guide* is not invulnerable and the West End production remains a classic example of how it can be done wrong. Where the ICA production had been low-key fringe theatre, cleverly making a virtue out of its scanty budget and minimal special effects, the Rainbow production was a huge, overblown rock opera.

The Rainbow, long since closed (in fact the failure of this show contributed to its demise) was a 1930s building which in the late 1970s had become more of a rock venue than a theatre. This, combined with the presence of a live rock group providing incidental music, led some reviewers to inaccurately label the production as a musical.

Mike Cule - who played at various times Prostetnic Vogon Jeltz, Deep Thought, Hotblack Desiato's bodyguard, the Dish of the Day, the Captain of the 'B' Ark and the voice of a mouse - remembers the opening night with horror: "Backstage was a little chaotic. They were still making my Vogon costume when I put it on, and the second half hadn't had a technical rehearsal." It didn't help that the actors playing Ford and Arthur had swapped roles with each other only a week before.

Two thousand *Hitchhiker's Guide* fans - almost three times as many as had seen the entire run of the ICA production - were treated to a show which could most charitably be described as long. Adapted, like the ICA version, from the radio scripts, the Rainbow production had kept in all those elements which the previous play had deleted or minimised. Consequently, the show was more than three hours long, a problem exacerbated by the band's insistence on performing an entire 35-minute set during the Milliways scene. By the time the curtain fell, well after midnight, all but the hardiest of the audience had long since departed.

"I saw the productions at the ICA, Clwyd and the Rainbow," said radio producer Geoffrey Perkins. "The ICA had the incredible hovercraft which to a certain extent covered up the details of the show which were a little rough. The Rainbow production of course was a disaster, which lost all the detail of Douglas' writing."

The critics tore the show to shreds, and although drastic measures were taken to cut the script and tighten up the production, the audience rapidly dwindled away to almost nothing. When the show finally closed, five weeks into its projected eight-week run, it was regularly playing to audiences of 50 or 60 - ironically smaller than those who had sat on the ICA's hovercraft! The producers disappeared, owing cast, crew and venue considerable amounts of money. Nobody would ever be crazy enough to stage *The Hitchhiker's Guide To The Galaxy* as a spectacular again. From now on, productions would stick to enthusiasm and a lot of imagination, best exemplified by the now standard technique of representing the council bulldozer with a Tonka toy.

Aside from the terrible reviews and chaotic opening night, the Rainbow production was memorable for two innovations. It was one of the first ever West End shows to incorporate lasers, much to the concern of the GLC Health and Safety Department. It also saw the first ever appearance of the Dish of the Day, the specially bred ruminant who wants to be eaten.

Two of the cast went on to appear in the TV series: Mike Cule as the Vogon Guard in Episode Two and David Learner inside the Marvin costume. Kim Durham (Arthur) was a regular on the SF soap *Jupiter Moon* and was also in *The Tripods* and a *Blake's 7* radio play.

Inbetween these two extremes, came the first provincial production of *Hitchhiker's Guide*, which was also the only stage version ever to tour.

# The Theatr Clwyd Productions

Dates: January-February 1980
Venues: Theatres in Bangor, Aberystwyth, Cardiff and Mold
Director: Jonathan Petherbridge
Cast included: Roger Blake, Mike Burns, David Learner

Like the Rainbow production, the Theatr Clwyd version was adapted fairly literally from the radio scripts, this time by Jonathan Petherbridge. Unlike the West End disaster, however, this version was produced by people who knew how reluctant most people would be to sit through a three-hour SF comedy. Petherbridge's solution was to stage two episodes each night on Tuesday, Wednesday and Thursday, then perform the whole six-part play for the hard-core fans on Friday and Saturday.

The most memorable element of the Theatr Clwyd production by far was the Haggunenon. While the subsequent TV series would shy away from showing a pilot's chair mutating into a carbon copy of the Ravenous Bugblatter Beast of Traal, Petherbridge felt that this was precisely the sort of effect which could not only be achieved on the stage of a small Welsh theatre, but could then be packed away and easily transported to other small Welsh theatres. The result was a huge inflatable Haggunenon - once seen, never forgotten - which was later loaned out to other stage productions preferring to follow the original storyline.

Greeted with both critical and popular acclaim, Petherbridge later shortened his script into a manageable two-act play, which subsequently became the standard stage version, although it was never actually published. The Theatr Clwyd 'Special Edition' toured England and Wales in late 1981. Starting at Theatr Clwyd's base in Mold in October, it travelled to Cambridge, Newcastle upon Tyne, Cardiff, Bristol, Stirling, Poole, Warwick and Swansea before finishing its run in December at Oxford Playhouse.

From the original production Roger Blake and David Learner reprised their roles as The Book and Marvin, having suffered the Rainbow fiasco in the interim. Also in the cast were Jon Strickland, Mike Burns, Harriet Keevil, Lewis Cowen, Andy Whitfield, Leader Hawkins, Tony Welch, Lizzi Cocker and Ken Ellis. Ellis, a professional puppeteer, was an unusual Zaphod in that his second head spent much of its time held in his right hand.

## More Professional Productions

*Hitchhiker's Guide* next appeared in the Drum studio at the Theatre Royal, Plymouth (May-June 1982) again directed by Jonathan Petherbridge, and with David Learner making his fourth and last stage appearance as Marvin. Linda Dobell was the first actress to play the book (the ICA's twin usherettes notwithstanding), a casting decision which later became something of a tradition, largely because there is only one other female role in the play. The other cast members included Simon Coady, Bev Willis, John Halford, Linda Jean-Barry, Jim Findley, David Kincaid and Stephen Mackenna

Still innovating, Petherbridge staged the Milliways scene in the Theatre Royal's bar, but after complaints from patrons attending the main theatre's production of *Jesus Christ Superstar*, the scene was moved back into the studio.

Derby Playhouse was the next venue to stage the Petherbridge adaptation (September-October 1982), this time directed by Christopher Honer. David Ericsson, Trevor Nichols, Keith Woodhams, Andy Readman, Tom Bowles, Hazel Ellerby (Chloe White in *Peak Practice*), Will Tacey, Michael Gunn and David Goodland comprised the cast of this version, which featured a radio-controlled Zaphod head.

The show was next presented at the Belgrade Theatre, Coventry (June-July 1983) in a production of the Petherbridge script directed by Rob Bettinson. The cast included Bill Stewart, Nicholas Geake, Jeffrey Chiswick, Leila Bertrand, Michael Mears (Cooper in *Sharpe*) and Peter Corey (Freddie Spence in *Brookside*). Lewis Cowen, who had played small roles for the Rainbow and Theatre Clwyd, finally came to the fore as The Book.

Finally, the one and only overseas professional production was staged at the La Boite Theatre in Brisbane, Australia from October to December 1983, proving so popular that its run was extended by a week. The script by Daniel Murphy was an original adaptation taking in elements of both the Rainbow script and the Petherbridge adaptation. For simplicity's sake, Zaphod was given only one head and two arms.

Unfortunately, by this time plans were well under way for the feature film version, and as is common with film rights, the picture's 'in development' status precluded any professional stage productions. Even more unfortunately, the film has remained 'in development' to this day, and until it is finally made and released, there will be no more professional theatrical productions of *The Hitchhiker's Guide To The Galaxy*. However, that clause in the film contract does not hamper the amateur dramatic scene.

## Amateur Productions

It is believed that the first ever amateur stage production of *The Hitchhiker's Guide To The Galaxy* was actually American, performed by students at a school in Hanover, New Hampshire, some time in the autumn of 1982. Lacking access to the Petherbridge version or the radio scripts, the play was adapted directly from the novel.

The Theatr Clwyd inflatable Haggunenon reappeared in a production at the Crescent Theatre, Birmingham, in February and March 1985, the same year that *Hitchhiker's Guide* was performed by students at Haywards Heath College, Sussex. A version performed by RATS (Redditch Amateur Theatrical Society) at the Palace Theatre, Redditch, in November 1986 also used the Haggunenon storyline, but kept the creature itself off stage. This production was also notable for a Marvin costume which was a large, silver-covered cardboard box, and for featuring a rare appearance by Lady Cynthia Fitzmelton, the civic dignitary who broke champagne on the bulldozers before they demolished Arthur's house in the first radio episode.

One of the most bizarre stage productions was that performed at the Comedia Colonia in Germany in February 1987, which was a one-man show! Axel Pape was the one man, and by all accounts the play was very entertaining. Two months later, a production at the Portsmouth Drama Centre, Southsea, established its own unique place in the field by incorporating scenes from the third and fourth novels, as well as a cameo appearance by Eccentrica Gallumbits, the triple-breasted whore of Eroticon VI (a character who, though mentioned, has never actually appeared in any other version of *Hitchhiker's Guide*).

The next production was at the Loft Theatre, Leamington Spa, in December 1988, while 1990 saw two am-dram versions: one by the Romsey Operatic and Dramatic Society, and one by the Menlo Players Guild of California, who enjoyed the experience so much that they staged the play again in 1994.

In May 1992, the Jonathan Petherbridge adaptation resurfaced in, of all places, Bermuda. Most impressively, the audience on the opening night of the Bermuda Musical and Dramatic Society's production included Prince Edward, who was touring the Caribbean at the time! (Interestingly, it was rumoured, during the Rainbow production's brief run, that Prince Andrew was in the audience one night.)

Always popular with students, *Hitchhiker's Guide* was performed at Liverpool John Moore's University in December 1994 and at Barry Boys' School, South Wales, in March 1995. In June 1996, children at Wildern School, Southampton who had been studying the novel in English lessons produced their own dramatised version from scratch in less than a week as an end of term project.

The Strathclyde Theatre Company in October 1996 performed an adaptation of the radio scripts on stage as a radio play, standing around microphones and even wearing BBC-style evening dress! A half-hour extract was performed at the University of Hawaii in April 1999, and there have been two recent productions in German: one in Linz, Austria, in 1998; the other by a group of German students at Brechtbau in February 2000 and again at Freiberg in May.

Possibly the oddest stage version of all was that performed by the Arena Theatre Company at the Regent Centre, Christchurch, Dorset, in May 1995. This was the much threatened 'musical version' with the cast breaking into a variety of 1960s pop songs, such as 'Don't They Know It's The End Of The World?' The result, apparently, was dire.

# 4: The Books

In early April 1978, as the first broadcast of the first series of *Hitchhiker's Guide* was drawing to a close, Douglas Adams started casting around for a publisher interested in turning his story into book form. "We had a rather infamous letter from BBC Enterprises turning down the chance to do a book or a record," recalled producer Geoffrey Perkins. "Really, the show was made as an absolute, outside-of-the-mainstream, fringe thing; everybody agreed that it was great, but nobody expected it to be a big success."

But a big success it was and Pan Books were prepared to offer Douglas Adams a £1,500 advance for the book, to be published in Autumn 1979, which he gratefully accepted. In May 1978, as the first radio series enjoyed its first set of repeats, BBC Publications wrote to Adams enquiring about the possibility of the book rights, and were rather shocked to discover that they were too late!

## *The Hitchhiker's Guide To The Galaxy*

Paperback: Pan Books, October 1979
Hardback: Arthur Barker Ltd, February 1980

*Story*: Arthur Dent wakes up, finds that his house is about to be knocked down, learns that his friend Ford Prefect is an alien and is rescued when the Vogons destroy Earth. Far away on the planet Damogran, Galactic President Zaphod Beeblebrox steals the fantastic *Heart Of Gold* spaceship which he is supposed to be launching.

Ford introduces Arthur to Babel fish, towels and *The Hitchhiker's Guide To The Galaxy*, but they are captured by the Vogons, tortured with poetry and thrown into space. Fortunately they are rescued by the *Heart Of Gold*, which is crewed by Zaphod, his girlfriend Trillian and Marvin the paranoid android.

Zaphod takes the *Heart Of Gold* to Magrathea, dormant home of a fabulously wealthy planet-building industry, and after a close shave involving two guided missiles, a bowl of petunias and a whale, the ship lands. Zaphod, Ford and Trillian go exploring, while Arthur meets Slartibartfast and Marvin stays by the ship.

Slartibartfast tells Arthur of the Earth's origins as a giant computer built by pan-dimensional beings (seen as mice) to find the question of life, the universe and everything after the great computer Deep Thought announced that the answer was 42. Trillian's white mice want to dissect Arthur's brain, but he makes his escape along with Ford, Zaphod and Trillian. They are cornered by two galactic cops, who are killed when their life-support systems blow up. Returning to the *Heart Of Gold*, they find that Marvin had talked the cops' shipboard computer into killing itself, and hence the cops.

Leaving Magrathea, the *Heart Of Gold* and its crew head for the restaurant at the end of the universe...

*Background*: *The Hitchhiker's Guide To The Galaxy* was written by Douglas Adams in late 1978 and the first half of 1979. By August 1979 (when *Hitchhiker's Guide* became the only radio series ever nominated for the World Science Fiction Award or 'Hugo,' losing out as Best Dramatic Presentation to *Superman: The Movie*), adverts were starting to appear, but there was no sign of the book.

The original plan had been for the novel to recount the storyline of the radio series, but in the end it only covered episodes one to four, and thus did not include any of John Lloyd's material from 'Fit The Fifth' and 'Fit The Sixth.' (Adams had originally considered co-writing the book with Lloyd, but subsequently opted to be sole author.) Legend tells how, as the print deadline loomed, an exasperated Pan executive told Adams to, "finish the page you're working on," before spiriting away the manuscript, glad to at least have something long enough to publish as a novel, even if it did seem to end rather abruptly.

An initial print run of 60,000 copies was ordered, and Pan's faith in the project was justified when the book entered the best-seller charts at number one. Within three months it had sold 250,000 copies. In January 1984, Douglas received a Golden Pan award from his publishers when paperback sales of the book broke one million.

*Comment*: For many people, the novel of *The Hitchhiker's Guide To The Galaxy* is their introduction to the story as a whole, and in many ways it is the definitive text. Certainly the radio series came first, but with the novel Douglas Adams was able to eliminate some of the less satisfactory parts of the story, and tidy up those which almost, but not quite, worked.

Given the chance to expand and reinvent the story from scratch, Adams goes off on wild flights of fancy into areas unexplored elsewhere in the *Hitchhiker's Guide* canon, such as the actual theft of the *Heart Of Gold*. It is worth reflecting that, when he wrote this, he cannot have imagined that 23 years later people would not only still be reading the book, but would still be listening to the radio series on which it was based and comparing the two.

This is one of those novels which can be returned to time and time again. The jokes that seemed so fresh and original on first reading turning into comfortably familiar friends. When returning to the novel after many years, there are many delights to be spotted, especially if you are familiar with the other versions. The footnote in Chapter 4, for example, mentions that only six people in the universe know where the real power lies, which ties in directly with 'Fit The Twelfth' (Adams wrote the novel and second radio series simultaneously).

## The Restaurant At The End Of The Universe

Paperback: Pan Books, October 1980
Hardback: Arthur Barker Ltd, February 1981

*Story*: Prostetnic Vogon Jeltz, in league with Zaphod's analyst Gag Halfrunt, is tracking the *Heart Of Gold*. As the Vogons move in to attack, Eddie the computer announces that all his circuits are taken up with Arthur's request for a cup of tea, so Zaphod organises a seance to contact his great-grand grandfather.

The ghost somehow causes the *Heart Of Gold* to leap out of danger while simultaneously making Arthur a pot of tea, but in the process Zaphod and Marvin disappear. Zaphod reappears outside the offices of *The Hitchhiker's Guide To The Galaxy*, aware that he has to find a man called Zarniwoop. He bumps into Marvin on the way to Zarniwoop's office, then meets Roosta as the building is attacked by Frogstar fighters. Marvin distracts then destroys a giant robot while Zaphod and Roosta escape but the whole building is torn from its foundations and taken to Frogstar World B.

Zaphod meets Gargravarr, custodian of the Total Perspective Vortex, who explains how the planet's population mutated into birds after passing the Shoe Event Horizon. After surviving the Total Perspective Vortex's torture because it merely panders to his ego, Zaphod finds a derelict spaceport where one ship still works. When the passengers wake up and panic, Zaphod retreats to the cockpit where he meets... Zarniwoop.

Zarniwoop switches off his artificial universe and Zaphod discovers that the *Heart Of Gold* was actually miniaturised and in his pocket all along. Reunited with Ford, Trillian and Arthur, Zaphod asks Eddie the computer to send them to the nearest place to eat, whereupon the four of them disappear in a puff of smoke.

They appear in Milliways, 'The Restaurant At The End Of The Universe,' where Ford meets an old friend, rock star Hotblack Desiato who is spending a year dead for tax reasons, and Arthur is revolted by an animal that wants to be eaten. Marvin telephones them from the car park, having stayed on Frogstar World B for 576,000,000,000 years. They go down there to meet him, and he helps them steal an extremely black spaceship.

Unable to control the ship, they discover that it belongs to Hotblack's band, Disaster Area, and is programmed to crash into a star. Marvin operates the emergency teleport, allowing the others to escape. Arthur and Ford materialise on the Golgafrinchan 'B' Ark which then crashes into a planet. The Golgafrinchans name it Fintlewoodlewix but Arthur and Ford find Slartibartfast's signature on a glacier and realise that they are on prehistoric Earth, which can now never function as it should. Resigned to their fate, they wander off to explore the planet.

*Background*: *The Restaurant At The End Of The Universe* was a direct sequel to *The Hitchhiker's Guide To The Galaxy*. With the first novel having ended so abruptly, a follow-up was inevitable and like its predecessor this book topped the best-seller charts. Ostensibly adapted from episodes five to twelve of the radio series, it is in fact based largely on 'Fit The Fifth' and 'Fit The Sixth', with the Disaster Area storyline replacing John Lloyd's Haggunenon sequence and disparate sequences from 'The Secondary Phase' integrated into the plot.

By April 1988, the paperback had sold one million copies and Douglas was awarded a second Golden Pan.

*Comment*: In many ways, this is the most satisfying of the five *Hitchhiker's Guide* novels. What could have been merely the final chapters of *The Hitchhiker's Guide To The Galaxy* is expanded into a book which takes the reader all over the universe, reinvents ideas from the entirety of the radio series and really fleshes out the characters, both principal and minor.

There is the same lightness of tone as the first book, but with a not unexpected maturity and confidence in the writing. The central Milliways sequence in particular is a joy to read, including the Dish of the Day scene which had originally been written for the Rainbow Theatre production.

The book finishes in the same place as the TV series and the first radio series, with Arthur and Ford on prehistoric Earth, a 'full circle' structure which brings the story to a completely satisfying conclusion. It is a testament to Adams' growing literary skills that he was able to incorporate into this storyline elements such as Zaphod's visit to the Total Perspective Vortex and the Man in the Shack, which followed afterwards in the radio series.

*The Restaurant At The End Of The Universe* is just the right length, just the right depth, and very, very funny. The only reason not to recommend this book as a starting point for those new to *Hitchhiker's Guide* is that, without having read the first book, it won't make sense.

# Life, The Universe And Everything

Paperback: Pan Books, August 1982
Hardback: Arthur Barker Ltd, September 1982

*Story*: After Arthur is insulted by an immortal being named Wowbagger the Infinitely Prolonged, he and Ford are transported to Lord's Cricket Ground where they meet Slartibartfast and witness a squad of deadly, cricket-playing robots steal the ashes. Marvin, who now has an artificial leg, meets a mattress called Zem but is then kidnapped by the cricket-playing robots. Trillian leaves Zaphod on the *Heart Of Gold*, which is then attacked by the robots, who shoot Zaphod and steal the Infinite Improbability Drive.

Ford and Arthur learn how the planet Krikkit existed inside a dust cloud so the inhabitants never knew there were any other stars or worlds; when the people of Krikkit finally discovered the galaxy, they decided to destroy it. Eventually defeated, Krikkit was locked in a time loop, the key to which was based on the galaxy's symbol of prosperity, the wicket. The key was blasted into pieces when a rogue Krikkit warship tried to seize it.

Slartibartfast, Arthur and Ford teleport into a flying party, searching for the silver bail but Arthur's teleport goes awry and he finds himself confronted by an aggrieved being called Agrajag who has been reincarnated many times, each time being accidentally killed by Arthur (including one time as a bowl of petunias). Agrajag tries to kill Arthur but dies again after revealing that Arthur will be nearly assassinated on Stavromula Beta.

Arthur falls off a mountain, accidentally learns to fly and gets hit by the party, where he meets Ford, Slartibartfast, Trillian and a man who won a Rory award for 'The Most Gratuitous Use Of The Word Fuck In A Serious Screenplay.' The robots appear and steal the Rory.

After the Krikkit robots release their planet from its time loop, the quartet descend to the planet where they find a confused population. Zaphod also sneaks down to Krikkit where he discovers that the robots have all become depressed because Marvin is plugged into their central computer.

Trillian correctly deduces that Krikkit has been controlled all along by a megalomaniac computer, Hactar, which once tried to destroy the universe but failed. Hactar was believed destroyed but in fact formed the dust cloud around Krikkit, which is now dispersed, saving the universe.

Arthur and Co. find a man called Prak who explains to them that simultaneous knowledge of the ultimate question and the ultimate answer is logically impossible. He also tells them where to find God's final message to His creation. Later, Arthur meets Wowbagger again.

*Background*: "After I wrote the second book I was utterly, completely determined that this was it - there would not be another *Hitchhiker* book,"

Douglas Adams told an interviewer, when *Life, The Universe And Everything* was published. "After the third one, I also say I'm not going to do another one."

For the first time, Pan promoted the book with extensive point of sale material, including the now infamous 'cans of everything' which were given away to reviewers and a few fortunate fans. On removing the ring-pull, each can proved to contain a slip of paper offering fabulous prizes via a lucky serial number, which was unfortunately printed in a type of ink which completely dissolves on contact with oxygen. It is known that at least one can remains sealed, its owner waiting for an opportunity to open it in a suitable vacuum chamber!

This book won Douglas Adams his third Golden Pan when sales passed one million copies. Mini-hardbacks of the first three *Hitchhiker's Guide* novels were published by Millennium in 1994, complete with a facsimile Douglas Adams signature.

Wowbagger the Infinitely Prolonged reappeared in 'The Private Life Of Ghengis Khan,' a short story in *The Utterly, Utterly Merry Comic Relief Christmas Book* in 1986. For a brief guide to discrepancies between the British and American editions of *Life, The Universe And Everything*, see Chapter 8.

*Comment*: Anybody expecting a novelisation of the second radio series (or rather, the bits of it not in *The Restaurant At The End Of The Universe*) was in for a surprise with this book. The only radio material was three lines of dialogue ("Imagine I have a Kill-O-Zap blaster in my hand..."). However, this wasn't a completely new story. It was a reworking of an unfilmed *Doctor Who* treatment, 'Doctor Who And The Krikkitmen,' which Adams had written long before *Hitchhiker's Guide*.

And frankly, you can tell. It's not that *Life, The Universe And Everything* is a bad book. It's a very good book - well-written and very funny. It's just not a *Hitchhiker's Guide To The Galaxy* book and it sits uneasily in the series, sandwiched inbetween the first two novels (young, fresh, exciting, adapted freely from the radio series) and the final two (mature, introspective, original). In particular, Slartibartfast seems out of place, a completely different character to the one in the first novel and the radio and TV series. The original Slartibartfast was a meek ditherer, but this one is dynamic and for some reason feels it's up to him to save the Universe.

There are some terrific ideas in *Life, The Universe And Everything*: Bistromathics, the flying party, and especially Agrajag. Agrajag is a superbly inventive way of explaining the first book's bowl of petunias gag which could have not only fallen flat but spoiled the original joke. It's a shame the character never reappeared in the later books. However, some characters, such as Judiciary Pag LIVR are not as memorable as they should be, and the whole climactic sequence with Prak fails to provide the sort of satisfying conclusion that the second book managed. Nor do Wowbagger the Infinitely Prolonged's book-ending cameos give the book a satisfying structure, being far too obvious an attempt to create a circular structure. The storyline as a whole is also slightly unsatisfying as the heroes spend most of the book chasing helplessly after the robots, failing to prevent them from reassembling the key.

Which is a shame because the book is in many other ways very enjoyable. It also has, in its original Pan paperback incarnation, easily the best cover of any *Hitchhiker's Guide* novel.

## *So Long And Thanks For All The Fish*

Hardback: Pan Books, November 1984
Paperback: Pan Books, November 1985

*Story*: After eight years of travelling through space and time, Arthur Dent returns home to Earth, and is rather alarmed to discover that he has arrived *after* the date on which he knows the planet was destroyed. He meets a truck driver, Rob McKenna, who is actually a rain god, and a young woman named Fenchurch, who had been sitting in a café in Rickmansworth on the day that the world was 'destroyed' - an event which is now put down to mass hallucination.

Arthur's home is as untidy as he left it, except that somebody has left him a beautifully made goldfish bowl, inscribed with the words, 'So long and thanks for all the fish.' Besotted by thoughts of Fenchurch, he meets her for a second time and discovers that she has the unusual capacity of walking very slightly above the ground, which prompts him to teach her how to fly.

Arthur learns that on the day when everyone imagined the world being destroyed, all the dolphins disappeared. He also discovers that Fenchurch has a fishbowl just like his. Together they travel to California to meet a man called Wonko the Sane, whose house is built inside out because he is convinced that the world is completely mad. Wonko also has a fishbowl.

It transpires that the world was saved from destruction by the dolphins, who somehow replaced it with an Earth from a parallel universe before making their farewells, leaving fishbowls as gifts.

Ford turns up, having escaped from the clutches of a Sirius Cybernetics Corporation rep, and sets off with Arthur and Fenchurch to see God's final message to His creation. On the way there, they discover Marvin, several times older than the universe and badly in need of repair. Together, the four travellers look on God's final message and are satisfied.

*Background*: Pan took a bold move with *So Long And Thanks For All The Fish*, which was published as the company's first ever mass-market hardback. The shiny black dust jacket carried a small 'lenticular' picture stuck to the front. Often incorrectly described as a 'hologram', this was not a 3D image but rather two completely different pictures. Viewed one way it showed a walrus, but tilted at an angle the image changed to a plesiosaur.

"There was no grand plan behind them," explained Adams many years later. "Someone from Pan Books happened to be in Hong Kong or maybe Japan and came across these little things and decided to buy up an industrial quantity of them and incorporate them into the design of *So Long*... I thought it worked very well and was very pleased with it. Inevitably a lot of people speculated on their significance and what I meant by them. Sadly, not long afterwards, a breakfast cereal company also bought a ton of them to give away in cereal packets, so the thing no longer seemed quite as idiosyncratic."

In 1988, the four *Hitchhiker's Guide* paperbacks were republished by Pan in a uniform edition. The covers were divided into quarters so that four different images could be created, depending on how the books were arranged: a red and white 'Don't Panic' towel; a Babel fish; a painting of the *Heart Of Gold* by acclaimed SF artist Chris Foss; and a computerised self-portrait of Douglas Adams. A mysterious pattern of coloured blobs on the books' spines revealed itself to be a colour-blindness test which showed the figure '42' - but not to everyone!

*Comment*: The most common reaction among *Hitchhiker's Guide* fans on reading *So Long And Thanks For All The Fish* was, "It's a bit slim, isn't it?" However nicely written it may be (and it is), however funny (it has some great moments), there simply isn't very much story. And a lot of what there is - Ford's solo adventures in trying to buy a drink, for example, or the whole Rob McKenna sub-plot - seems somewhat superfluous to the main Arthur/Fenchurch storyline.

As the first entirely original *Hitchhiker's Guide* novel, *So Long* feels more naturally constructed than *Life, The Universe And Everything*, with a strong beginning, a satisfying middle and a wry if inconclusive ending. It's just a shame that the three of them are so close together. Zaphod and Trillian are mentioned, but don't appear, and Marvin's function is little more than a cameo to please the fans. Adams even steps outside his narrative at one point to suggest that the less patient readers should flick straight to the final chapter, 'which is a good bit and has Marvin in it.'

Nevertheless, the book succeeds admirably in terms of retrospectively explaining and connecting aspects of the earlier story which were constructed originally as little more than comic asides, and readers unaware of the books' disparate genesis could well believe that Adams planned this all from the start.

Of the minor characters, Rob McKenna and Wonko the Sane are both memorable. And God's final message to His creation is a clever conceit which won't be revealed here.

## *'Young Zaphod Plays It Safe'*

*Story*: The Beeblebrox Salvage And Really Wild Stuff Corporation is employed by the Safety And Civil Reassurance Administration to track down a missing spaceship which should have delivered three deeply dangerous Sirius Cybernetics Corporation rejects into a black hole. The ship is found and one of the capsules is missing. The trajectory of the only escape pod is plotted and found to lead to a small planet in the sector ZZ9 Plural Z Alpha. The planet must be made 'perfectly safe'...

*Background*: In 1986, Douglas Adams became involved with the charity Comic Relief, for whom he co-edited with Peter Fincham (later executive producer of *Murder Most Horrid, I'm Alan Partridge*, etc.) a book of comedy material. Adams himself contributed three short stories to *The Utterly, Utterly Merry Comic Relief Christmas Book*, one and a half of which were *Hitchhiker's Guide To The Galaxy* related.

The semi-*Hitchhiker's Guide* story in the Comic Relief book was 'The Private Life Of Genghis Khan,' which Adams adapted from a TV sketch he had originally written with Graham Chapman in 1975. Adams added a cameo appearance by Wowbagger the Infinitely Prolonged, thus establishing the tale (in some people's view) as part of the *Hitchhiker's Guide* canon. The third Douglas Adams story in the book was 'A Christmas Fairly Story,' co-written with Terry Jones. 'The Private Life Of Genghis Khan' was posted on Douglas Adams' official Website some years later, and 'Young Zaphod' was included in various American omnibus editions of *Hitchhiker's Guide*, but 'A Christmas Fairly Story' has never been reprinted.

*Comment*: 'Young Zaphod Plays It Safe' remains the only absolutely 100% *Hitchhiker's Guide* short story ever published, although it left fans somewhat nonplussed, mainly because of the unclear ending. Just who was the mysterious being referred to at the story's close? Some people said it was (then US President) Ronald Reagan, while others maintained that it was Jesus Christ. When the story was republished in Peter Haining's anthology *The Wizards Of Odd* in 1996, the final line was changed to make it clear that the being is in fact Reagan, although the joke had by then of course lost all its topicality.

# Mostly Harmless

Hardback: Heinemann, October 1992
Paperback: Pan Books, October 1993

*Story*: Tricia McMillan, a successful TV journalist, regrets not having gone off with the 'guy from another planet' whom she once met at a party, so she is happy to accompany three aliens who invite her back to their home world, Rupert, the solar system's tenth planet.

Sneaking into the *Hitchhiker's Guide To The Galaxy* offices, Ford Prefect reprograms a security robot to be his happy servant. Ford learns that the new management, InfiniDim Enterprises, want to boost profits by spreading a multidimensional *Hitchhiker's Guide* across infinite universes and by marketing the new version at affluent businessmen. He knocks out the editor, steals his ID card, and reprograms the main *Hitchhiker's Guide* computer.

Arthur Dent travels listlessly and recklessly, having lost Fenchurch in a hyperspace accident but knowing he can never die until after he has been to Stavromula Beta.

Escaping InfiniDim security, Ford discovers that the *Hitchhiker's Guide* offices have a secret thirteenth floor, on which he finds the *Hitchhiker's Guide* Mk.2, a smooth, circular, buttonless black device. He also realises that InfiniDim is run by Vogons. To safeguard the prototype *Hitchhiker's Guide* Mk.2, he sends it to Arthur.

Arthur has finally found peace as a sandwich maker on the planet of the Perfectly Normal Beasts. Much to his surprise he is visited by Trillian, now a successful intergalactic journalist, and her teenage daughter, Random, conceived using Arthur's DNA from a sperm bank. Trillian leaves Arthur and Random to get to know each other.

Random opens the package which Arthur receives; the *Hitchhiker's Guide* Mk.2 explains to her about probabilities and parallel universes and shows her an alternative version of her mother arriving on Rupert. Random takes off in a spaceship. Searching for her, Arthur finds Ford, whose ship it was, and they follow the migrating Perfectly Normal Beasts through a dimensional portal to The Domain Of The King.

Back on Earth, Tricia McMillan is very surprised when a teenage daughter she didn't know she had turns up in a spaceship. At the Domain Of The King Bar And Grill, Arthur and Ford are given a spaceship by a singer and head to Earth, where they try to track down Tricia and Random, while the Vogons close in on the planet to finish a job they once started...

*Background*: With the fifth book in 'the increasingly inaccurately named *Hitchhiker's Trilogy*,' Douglas Adams' inability to hit deadlines really came to the fore. In January 1991, his new hardback publishers Heinemann announced that *Mostly Harmless* would be published in October of that year. In October they announced that the book would in fact be published in January 1992. By January the book remained unfinished and publication was rescheduled again, this time for July. In March 1992 Heinemann resorted to literally locking Douglas Adams in a hotel room until he finished the damn book. This was too late for a July publication, so the date was set at October 1992, when the book finally appeared, exactly one year late.

*Comment*: *Mostly Harmless* reads even less like a *Hitchhiker's Guide* novel than *Life, The Universe And Everything*. It is far more serious than the previous four and deals with weightier subjects in terms of parallel universes, yet it also lacks the grand, pangalactic conceits of the original story. In early *Hitchhiker's Guide*, Arthur was a hapless witness to the insanity around him, while Ford, Zaphod and Marvin hurtled around the universe, improbably interacting with things.

But *Mostly Harmless* is Arthur's personal story, along with the story of Trillian and Random. Trillian was never a fully fleshed-out character, but comes into her own here - in both versions of herself. Random just about manages to avoid being a stereotypical teenager.

The book suffers by alternating too frequently for too long between the three sub-plots - Arthur, Tricia McMillan and Ford - before they all bind together at the end. If anything, this book is most notable for Adams' updated version of *The Hitchhiker's Guide To The Galaxy*, which reflects his growing interest in communication technology. This is best summed up by an aside from the novel: 'A computer terminal is not some clunky old television with a typewriter in front of it. It is an interface where the mind and body can connect with the universe and move bits of it about.'

Incidentally, the idea that, when Zaphod first met Trillian at a fancy-dress party, his second head was disguised as a parrot in a covered cage, originated in the computer game. Zaphod does not actually appear in this book, nor do Marvin, Slartibartfast, Fenchurch or any of the other expected characters. There is, however, a teasingly slight reference to 42.

# 5: The Recordings

## *The Hitchhiker's Guide To The Galaxy*

Double LP or Double Cassette: Original Records, November 1979 (mail order), May 1980 (shops)

Cast: Peter Jones, Simon Jones, Geoffrey McGivern, Mark Wing-Davey, Cindy Oswin, Stephen Moore, Richard Vernon, Valentine Dyall, David Tate, Jim Broadbent, Bill Wallis

*Story*: The storyline of the double album approximately followed the first four episodes of the radio series, but with a few scenes deleted (for example, persuading Mr Prosser to lie in the mud) and other minor textual changes.

*Background*: "We spoke to a couple of record companies after BBC Enterprises turned us down," remembers producer Geoffrey Perkins. "We agreed, in principal, to make a record with one guy who, while we were considering the contract, insisted on showing us a hard-core porn film."

In the end, a deal was signed with Original Records, a small independent label which released two other comedy albums in 1981: *An Evening Without*, a collection of old Footlights sketches performed by Griff Rhys Jones, Clive Anderson and others, including two pieces written by Douglas Adams; and *439 Golden Greats*, a collection of pop spoofs by the HeeBee-GeeBees.

The principal radio cast were reassembled for the recording, with the exception of Susan Sheridan, who was working on the Disney film *The Black Cauldron*. Instead, Cindy Oswin from the ICA stage production was drafted in to play Trillian.

The album was first made available by mail order only although it was later released to record shops. However, by then most *Hitchhiker's Guide* fans had ordered the album, so sales were poor. *The Hitchhiker's Guide To The Galaxy* is possibly the best-selling record never to make the charts.

After the first batch of records and tapes had been produced, an old school friend of Douglas Adams' complained about the name given to the worst poet in the universe. Rather than bring back Peter Jones to record four words, Original Records simply cut up that part of the master tape and reassembled it in the wrong order, resulting in the garbled nonsense which has puzzled listeners ever since.

*Comment*: In retrospect, BBC Records' decision to pass up the chance to release *The Hitchhiker's Guide To The Galaxy* has a certain logic to it. As a six-part serial, it would have required three LPs, an enormous investment in something which, though popular, had yet to prove its longevity (the double cassette format for radio comedy was still unknown at this time).

Geoffrey Perkins summed up the differences between the album and the radio series when he said, "The radio series had been very low-tech, whereas the records were slightly more high-tech which meant that on the one hand we could do a few more things that we wanted, but possibly the show lost something because of it. But there were some great things about the records, such as Tim Souster's music, which was extraordinary."

## The Hitchhiker's Guide To The Galaxy Part Two - The Restaurant At The End Of The Universe

LP or Cassette: Original Records, November 1980

Cast: Peter Jones, Simon Jones, Geoffrey McGivern, Mark Wing-Davey, Cindy Oswin, Stephen Moore, Roy Hudd, Anthony Sharp, David Tate, Frank Middlemass, Stephen Grief, Loueen Willoughby, Graham de Wilde

*Story*: Ostensibly based on 'Fit The Fifth' and 'Fit The Sixth,' the inclusion of the Disaster Area storyline in place of the Haggunenon sequence actually made the two sides of this album more similar to the TV series episodes five and six (which were yet to be filmed). Whereas the previous album had cut about five minutes out of each episode's script, the second LP managed to actually be slightly longer than the two radio episodes on which it was based.

*Background*: One year later, the cast was reassembled to record a follow-up album. Stephen Grief (known to SF fans as Travis in *Blake's 7*) played three minor roles and later said, "My main memory of *Hitchhiker's Guide* is that I never got paid for it!"

The second album was released straight to the shops and reached number 47 in the charts, but overall sales were poorer than for its predecessor and it was eventually remaindered.

*Comment*: For some reason, *The Restaurant At The End Of The Universe* just doesn't have the same sparkle as the first album. It is too long and, being a follow-up, doesn't work on its own. However, at the time it looked unlikely that the radio series would ever be released so this was the only way to own the story in audio form. The album's poor reputation probably has more to do with its ubiquity in £1.99 remainder bins throughout the 1980s than its actual quality.

Whether the poor sales of the second *Hitchhiker's Guide* album contributed to the demise of Original Records is not known. What is known is that only the principal cast were paid. "I seem to remember getting paid a fee, small though it was, and getting absolutely no royalties," remembered Simon Jones. "But then of course they didn't sell any. They didn't seem to have any way of distributing them. The whole thing was a total mess."

Douglas Adams actually took out a lawsuit against Original Records in 1984, telling an interviewer, "They were originally just a little two-man outfit working out of a small studio. Then they put out the *Hitchhiker* albums and they are now in a suite of offices with secretaries and everything. I walked into their office and said, 'Heh, heh, heh, you're spending my royalties, aren't you?' To which they replied, 'Heh, heh, heh, of course we're not.'"

## The Theme Single

Seven-Inch Single: Original Records, January 1981

Most of the music on the two Original Records album was written and recorded by Tim Souster, although Paddy Kingsland (who oversaw the music in the first series and composed the music for the second) also contributed a few tracks. Souster also recorded a new version of the *Hitchhiker's Guide* theme, 'Journey Of The Sorcerer,' originally a track on the Eagles album *One Of These Nights*.

Two of the three tracks on the B-side of this single were from *The Restaurant At The End Of The Universe*: 'Reg Nullify In Concert,' a song by Graham de Wilde heard in the background at Milliways; and Peter Jones' narration on the rock band Disaster Area, without Souster's backing music. What really excited the fans, however, was the final track, 'Only The End Of The World Again' by Disaster Area, a completely new SF rock song featuring Douglas Adams himself on rhythm guitar!

## The Marvin Singles

'Marvin'/'Metal Man' Seven-Inch Single: Polydor, June 1981

'Reasons To Be Miserable'/'Marvin I Love You' Seven-Inch Single: Depressive Discs/Polydor, October 1981

The man behind these singles was John Sinclair, producer of hit records for every band from Foreigner to Buggles, and an old friend of Stephen Moore.

"He was very much into what he called 'the theatre of wax' which meant doing dramatic things on record, with music," recalls Moore. "We did the first record and we were happy with it, and we said, 'Look, we can't not involve Douglas.' So Douglas came round and he had lots of ideas - which we listened to very politely! Then we said, 'Thanks. We'll put your name on the credits anyway, if that's alright with you.' And he was quite happy with that."

'Marvin' was released just as *Hitchhiker's Guide* fever was at its peak, with the TV series and the radio series both being repeated and *The Restaurant At The End Of The Universe* still selling well in bookshops. It was played frequently by Terry Wogan on Radio 2 and Marvin even mimed to the song on *Blue Peter*! All this publicity took the record to the heady chart heights of number 53, enough to make Marvin the only robot ever listed in *The Guinness Book Of British Hit Singles*.

As a follow-up, Moore and Sinclair recorded two further songs – a record also known as 'The Double B-Side' - again giving an honorary credit to Adams. But public interest in *Hitchhiker's Guide* was by now on the wane, a situation not helped by the cancellation of the second TV series. The record failed to make the top 75 and rapidly became a collector's item. (There has been some speculation that the female vocals on 'Marvin I Love You' are by Sandra Dickinson, but it is just a session singer.)

What has remained largely unknown until now is that Stephen Moore and John Sinclair recorded a third Marvin single, a Christmas song. However, the failure of 'The Double B-Side' resulted in Polydor losing interest in the project and the single never even made it as far as a final mix. It is unlikely that this will ever be heard because the copyright situation after all this time will be extremely complex.

## The Abridged Talking Books

*The Hitchhiker's Guide To The Galaxy*, Double Cassette: Listen For Pleasure, November 1981

*The Restaurant At The End Of The Universe*, Double Cassette: Listen For Pleasure, April 1983

*Life, The Universe And Everything*, Double Cassette: Listen For Pleasure, October 1984

*So Long And Thanks For All The Fish*, Double Cassette: Listen For Pleasure, September 1985

*Background*: Talking Books were just starting to become popular in the early 1980s when Listen For Pleasure, a budget label owned by EMI, released the four (as was) *Hitchhiker's Guide* novels all read by Stephen Moore. Four books in this format by one author was unprecedented and the tapes sold incredibly well, only being deleted in the early 1990s when they were supplanted by unabridged readings. Producer Barry McCann abridged the text of each book to a running time of approximately two hours. Moore tried where he could to match the voices of the characters as they had been on the radio.

*Comment*: Although the unabridged readings have since supplanted these ones, they are still worth listening to. Stephen Moore is an excellent reader and the abridgements are sensitive and well done.

## The Unabridged Talking Books

*The Hitchhiker's Guide To The Galaxy*, Four Cassettes: Isis Audio Books, April 1994, Four CDs: Isis Audio Books, November 1994

*The Restaurant At The End Of The Universe*, Four Cassettes: Isis Audio Books, April 1994

*Life, The Universe And Everything*, Four Cassettes: Isis Audio Books, May 1994

*So Long And Thanks For All The Fish*, Four Cassettes: Isis Audio Books, May 1994

*Mostly Harmless*, Four Cassettes: Isis Audio Books, June 1994

*Background*: Dove Audio, one of the leading producers of spoken word recordings in the USA, acquired the rights to *The Hitchhiker's Guide To The Galaxy* and its sequels in 1990 and asked Douglas Adams himself to read them. The results ran to approximately six hours each and were spread over four cassettes per book. In 1994, Isis Audio Books acquired the UK rights to these recordings, releasing them singly and as a five-book, 20-cassette pack.

*Comment*: With his experience of performing in Footlights, Douglas Adams had no problem in providing dramatic readings of his own works. These can be regarded as the definitive readings, and the first was even nominated for a Grammy. However, some UK listeners were undoubtedly puzzled to find that the audio version of *Life, The Universe And Everything* was the American one, with its numerous alterations (see Chapter 8).

*The Hitchhiker's Guide To The Galaxy* broke new ground yet again when it became the first unabridged audio book to be released on compact disc, initially in a signed limited edition of 1,600. Unfortunately, *The Restaurant At The End Of The Universe* is a slightly longer book and simply could not be fitted onto four CDs. Isis were reluctant to edit the recording, but were equally unhappy about releasing it as five discs, and so the problem remains.

## The Radio Series

Ten years after it was broadcast, and with the Original Records versions deleted, the BBC finally released the original radio series of *The Hitchhiker's Guide To The Galaxy* in September 1988. It was available as a boxed set of either six cassettes or six compact discs, the first BBC radio programme to be released in CD format.

There was one minor cut in the programme, in 'Fit The Third' when Marvin hums 'Shine On You Crazy Diamond' by Pink Floyd, as the BBC was unable to obtain permission to use the song. All the other music used in the first series, by artists such as Fripp and Eno, Jean-Michel Jarre and Tomita, was cleared for release, including the Eagles' version of 'Journey Of The Sorcerer' and the traditional closing theme, Louis Armstrong singing 'What A Wonderful World.'

In 1993 the series was re-released as two double cassettes with series one renamed 'The Primary Phase' and 'Fit The Seventh' plus series two called 'The Secondary Phase.' CD reissues under these titles appeared in 1997 as two three-disc packs, and the tapes were reissued again in new packaging in March 1998 to mark the show's twentieth anniversary, followed shortly afterwards by a cassette-only release of the documentary *The Guide To Twenty Years' Hitchhiking* as *Douglas Adams' Guide To The Hitchhiker's Guide To The Galaxy*, which also included a lengthy interview with Adams.

# 6: The Television Series

## Episode 1

First broadcast: 5th January 1981

Cast: Peter Jones, Simon Jones, David Dixon, Joe Melia, Martin Benson, Steve Conway, Cleo Rocos, Andrew Mussell

*Story*: Arthur Dent finds that his house is about to be knocked down and learns that his friend Ford Prefect is an alien. Ford and Arthur escape from the Earth just as the Vogons blow it up, but are captured and threatened with poetry.

## Episode 2

First broadcast: 12th January 1981

Cast: Peter Jones, Simon Jones, David Dixon, Mark Wing-Davey, Sandra Dickinson, Stephen Moore, David Learner, Martin Benson, Michael Cule, David Tate, Rayner Bourton, Gil Morris

*Story*: Arthur and Ford are subjected to Prostetnic Vogon Jeltz's poetry, then thrown into space where they are rescued by the *Heart Of Gold*, on board which they find the improbable crew of Zaphod Beeblebrox, Trillian and Marvin.

## Episode 3

First broadcast: 19th January 1981

Cast: Peter Jones, Simon Jones, David Dixon, Mark Wing-Davey, Sandra Dickinson, Stephen Moore, David Learner, David Tate, Richard Vernon

*Story*: In orbit around Magrathea, Arthur saves the day by improbably turning two missiles into a bowl of petunias and a whale. On the planet, Ford, Zaphod and Trillian explore underground, while Arthur and Marvin stay on the surface. Arthur meets Slartibartfast, who takes him underground to show him the Earth Mk.2.

## Episode 4

First broadcast: 26th January 1981

Cast: Peter Jones, Simon Jones, David Dixon, Mark Wing-Davey, Sandra Dickinson, Richard Vernon, Anthony Carrick, Timothy Davies, David Leland, Charles McKeown, Marc Smith, Valentine Dyall, Matt Zimmerman

*Story*: Arthur watches recordings of the day Deep Thought was switched on and the day it proclaimed the answer to life, the universe and everything to be 42, and he learns about the origins of the Earth and the significance of mice. Trillian's mice, Frankie and Benjy, want to dissect Arthur's brain, but the cops arrive searching for Zaphod and in the confusion Arthur, Ford, Zaphod and Trillian escape. They cower behind a computer bank, which explodes...

## Episode 5

First broadcast: 2nd February 1981

Cast: Peter Jones, Simon Jones, David Dixon, Mark Wing-Davey, Sandra Dickinson, Stephen Moore, David Learner, Peter Davison, Jack May, Colin Jeavons, Dave Prowse, Barry Frank Warren, Colin Bennett

*Story*: ...depositing them at Milliways, which was built on the ancient ruins of Magrathea. Ford says hello to Hotblack Desiato and Arthur is repulsed by the talking Dish of the Day. Marvin telephones them from the car park and they head down there, where they steal an extremely black spaceship. Unfortunately, it cannot be controlled from on board and is programmed to fly into a star.

## Episode 6

First broadcast: 9th February 1981

Cast: Peter Jones, Simon Jones, David Dixon, Mark Wing-Davey, Sandra Dickinson, Stephen Moore, David Learner, Rayner Bourton, Aubrey Morris, Beth Porter, Matthew Scurfield, David Neville, Geoffrey Beevers, David Rowlands, Jon Glover

*Story*: Marvin stays on board the Disaster Area stuntship, allowing Ford, Arthur, Zaphod and Trillian to escape by teleport. Ford and Arthur materialise on the Golgafrinchan 'B' Ark which shortly afterwards crashes into and colonises Fintlewoodlewix. Arthur and Ford recognise the planet as prehistoric Earth and realise that its programming is now flawed. Resigned to their fate, they wander off to explore the planet.

*Background*: As early as 1978, while Douglas Adams was writing the novel of *The Hitchhiker's Guide To The Galaxy*, consideration was being given to a TV version. Initially the suggestion was made that the series be animated, but this was never followed up. The real starting point of the *Hitchhiker's Guide* TV series was a memo from John Lloyd to the BBC Head of Light Entertainment in September 1979. Lloyd would go on to be credited as Executive Producer on the pilot episode and Associate Producer on episodes 2-6, although his work on the hugely successful satire series *Not The Nine O'Clock News* meant that his input to the later episodes was minimal. He also received an 'Additional Material' credit for episode 5, relating back to his work on the original radio scripts.

The first task in producing the TV series was to appoint a producer. Alan JW Bell had directed two episodes of Michael Palin and Terry Jones' series *Ripping Yarns*, as well as comedy sketches for cult 1970s kids' series *Crackerjack*, and has since become the regular director of the inordinately long-running and successful sitcom *Last Of The Summer Wine*. With no experience in science fiction or the more 'alternative' aspects of TV comedy, Bell was very much of the BBC old school. While his workmanlike attitude and level-headedness undoubtedly helped to bring the show in on schedule and within the budget, there was a definite clash of personalities between Bell and the Oxbridge young guns.

Bell received Douglas Adams' pilot script in January 1980, around the same time that Adams was waxing enthusiastic to interviewers about the prospects of the animation which he envisaged as accompanying the narration sequences: "What you can do just with computer diagrams and computer graphics is immensely exciting."

Indeed it was, but it was also incredibly crude and blocky, making it difficult to get over the sort of subtle, throw-away visual gags that a series like *Hitchhiker's Guide* demanded. This was the era of the Acorn Atom and the ZX80 and smooth, scrolling computer animation was unknown to anyone without access to a Cray supercomputer.

The problem was solved by a chance meeting between Bell and a teenage animator named Kevin Davies which gave Bell the opportunity to ask an actual science fiction fan what he thought of a TV adaptation of *Hitchhiker's Guide*. Davies was already a massive fan of the series, and his enthusiasm not only persuaded Bell to take the producer's job, but also gave Davies' employer, Pearce Studios, the chance to bid for and win the opportunity to create the TV series' graphics.

It should be stressed at this point (and will be again) that NO COMPUTERS WERE USED IN THE CREATION OF THE TV SERIES GRAPHICS. The whole of every single animated sequence was created using traditional cel animation techniques, just like any cartoon. Not only do certain erroneous publications and ill-informed authors persist in spreading this myth, but occasionally unscrupulous computer graphics artists have even dishonestly claimed credit for the animation.

Although Peter Jones' narration was virtually identical to that used in the radio series, it was recorded anew. Animator Rod Lord and his team then printed out the text and accompanying graphical images in negative on plastic cels. Coloured gels were placed behind the cels which were photographed on a lightbox. Animation and text were made to gradually appear by placing a solid black cel on top and sliding it slightly (one letter at a time) as each new frame was photographed.

Several of the radio cast were retained for the TV series, with Simon Jones and Mark Wing-Davey returning to the roles which had been based on them in the first place. However, Ford Prefect was recast from original actor (and inspiration) Geoffrey McGivern to David Dixon. American actress Sandra Dickinson, who was married at the time to the actor then playing Doctor Who, Peter Davison, took the role of Trillian. Stephen Moore was offered the chance to play Marvin, but elected to only supply the voice and so the costume was filled by David Learner, who had played the role on stage.

The other two actors from the radio series to transfer to television in the same roles were Richard Vernon as Slartibartfast and David Tate as the voice of Eddie the computer. Valentine Dyall, the radio series' Gargravarr, provided the voice of Deep Thought as he had for the LP version, while Michael Cule, who had played numerous roles in the Rainbow Theatre production, achieved his aim of landing the Vogon Guard role.

Jim Francis, a veteran of *Blake's 7* and *Doctor Who*, was called on at short notice to design and build the many special effects required, including the Marvin costume. Zaphod's second head, designed and operated by effects technician Mike Kelt was given limited (radio-controlled) movement, but was generally held to be less than successful, more because of time constraints than budget. Mark Wing-Davey was slightly aggrieved to discover that the head actually cost more than he did! Zaphod's third arm was either tucked, Napoleon-style, into the character's jacket or provided by Kelt standing behind Wing-Davey.

Cheap though the series looks in retrospect, it was actually extremely expensive, sapping almost the entire effects budget of the Light Entertainment department for 1980. One result of this was that the BBC could not afford to make a series of *The Goodies* that year, which precipitated that trio's move to London Weekend Television.

The pilot was recorded in May and June 1980. In order to persuade the BBC that it genuinely was funny, a screening was arranged at the National Film Theatre to which a hundred or so science fiction fans were invited, their response being added as a laughter track. For this screening, Peter Jones recorded a special introduction, his only on-screen appearance for *Hitchhiker's Guide*, which was later included in *The Making Of The Hitchhiker's Guide To The Galaxy*. The pilot episode received two other public preview screenings: at the Edinburgh Television Festival and at Hitchercon 1, the first ever *Hitchhiker's Guide To The Galaxy* convention.

With the BBC persuaded that the series could work, production on the remaining five episodes ran from September 1980 through to January 1981, with the final special effects footage for episode 6 being shot three days after the first episode went on air.

Locations used in the series included a clay pit in Cornwall as Magrathea and a hillside in Lancashire as Prehistoric Earth. Arthur's house and the nearby pub were both in Sussex. Most of the sets were constructed at Television Centre in London, where the infamous revolving stage from *Blankety Blank* was redressed to become the bridge of the *Heart Of Gold*. The ambitious Milliways set was the largest set ever constructed at Television Centre.

The scenes featuring Deep Thought were shot at Ealing, while the explosion of a Magrathean computer bank was actually shot on a set built outside (on a golf course) for safety reasons. Matte paintings were used to create both the interior of the Vogon ship and the pier at Southend, while some of the Vogon corridors were actually redressed set elements from the film *Alien*.

Although the series was finished on schedule, time constraints were very tight and several scenes were either not filmed or filmed but subsequently cut. One shot of Arthur Dent was actually spare footage of Simon Jones running across the studio to shoot another scene! One of the cut scenes involved Arthur finding a silver costume in his quarters on the *Heart Of Gold* - although it is now accepted that Arthur spends the entire story dressed in his dressing gown and pyjamas, this was never actually stated in either the radio series or the novel.

First broadcast as six 35-minute episodes, the series was trimmed to fit a 30-minute slot from its first repeat and the excised scenes (such as Arthur and Ford in the Vogon airlock) were only restored when the series was released on video in May 1992. This video release, which had actually been prepared for a proposed videodisc release in the early 1980s, also added a very small amount of previously unseen footage, but removed all credits except the opening title sequence of Episode 1 and the closing credits of Episode 6.

*Comment*: Two decades on, the TV series of *The Hitchhiker's Guide To The Galaxy* still passes one crucial test - it's still funny. The cast are good and the script is witty. But it is the animated graphics which most people remember and which deservedly won the bulk of the series' acclaim. It says something about the animation's sophistication that many published sources mistakenly describe it as 'an early example of computer graphics' (it also says something about the amount of research that goes into some books on cult television!). In actual fact, computer graphics in 1980 were still extremely primitive and even with the most sophisticated computers available (and a huge budget), the BBC's own graphics department could never have produced animation as complex as this.

Where the series is let down, as many critics have observed, is in the special effects. The spaceships are crudely matted against the backgrounds; the wires supporting Slartibartfast's air car are obvious; and Zaphod's second head is slightly less lifelike than Torchy the Battery Boy. But the series must be seen within its historical context. Effective, impressive science fiction special effects were limited at this time to Hollywood movies such as *Star Wars* and would not make inroads into television until several years later. When *The Hitchhiker's Guide To The Galaxy* was produced, even American television could not produce anything more impressive by way of special effects than *Battlestar Galactica* or *Buck Rogers In The 25th Century*. Given the minuscule resources of BBC TV, the effects on *Hitchhiker's Guide* were, if not better, at least better value for money.

The design work in the TV series met with mixed reactions, and still does. Stephen Moore in particular disliked the Marvin costume and declined to wear it, leaving a vacancy for David Learner to recreate his role from the stage production. But as Visual Effects Designer Jim Francis observed, "One of the hardest people to please was Douglas Adams. He'd never really visualised what the *Heart Of Gold* looked like, what Marvin looked like, or anything looked like. It was all just in words. But when you put something in front of him, he'd just go, 'No, it's not like that, that's not how I see it.'"

Despite all this, the TV series of *Hitchhiker's Guide* still works on many levels. Where contemporary shows may now be the subject of mockery, *The Hitchhiker's Guide To The Galaxy* has survived precisely because it sets out to mock. As a spoof on science fiction, and as a SF-based spoof on reality, the series succeeded in 1981 and it still succeeds today.

Inflation being what it is, one of the show's funniest lines is now the barman's astonishment at Ford Prefect's generosity when buying six pints: "Keep the change." "What? From a fiver? Thank you, sir."

# The Making Of
# The Hitchhiker's Guide To The Galaxy

The importance of Kevin Davies in the history of *The Hitchhiker's Guide To The Galaxy* cannot be understated. He sculpted and operated props and masks for the Rainbow Theatre production, he was directly responsible for Pearce Studios providing the TV series' animated graphics, and later he oversaw the creation of *The Illustrated Hitchhiker's Guide To The Galaxy*. In between, he produced *The Making Of The Hitchhiker's Guide To The Galaxy* for BBC video.

Being a massive fan of *Hitchhiker's Guide* since he first heard the radio version, Davies took full advantage of his access to the set of the TV series, on the second half of which he was actually given a series of spoof credits: 'Mouse Trainer,' 'Milliways Catering' and 'Bath Superintendent.' Davies took many photographs on the set and even shot some home video footage.

In 1992, he persuaded BBC Enterprises that this unseen footage could be incorporated into a documentary about the making of the TV series. Interviews with Douglas Adams and others were shot in October of that year, together with new dramatised scenes filmed on location at 'Arthur Dent's house' in Sussex. (Davies reused this innovative semi-dramatisation technique for his subsequent documentary on *Doctor Who*, *30 Years In The TARDIS*, which also included comments from Douglas Adams.)

Peter Jones, Simon Jones, David Dixon and Mike Cule recreated their roles for the documentary, and the original Vogon guard and Marvin costumes were located and used. Although it sold well on video (including an American release), *The Making Of The Hitchhiker's Guide To The Galaxy* has not yet been broadcast on television.

## The Second Television Series

When the TV version proved to be a success, the obvious question raised was whether there would be a second series. Mark Wing-Davey said in an interview that the second series would start at a cricket match, suggesting that Douglas Adams was considering basing the script on his unused *Doctor Who* treatment, 'Doctor Who And The Krikkitmen.' However, the complexities and expense of the first series meant that a second series was deemed non-viable and it was confirmed cancelled in November 1981, just as publication of a third novel was announced. Geoffrey Perkins summed up the problems when he said, "I was asked to be script editor of the putative second TV series, but I turned it down on the grounds that the absolutely worst job in the world was trying to get a script out of Douglas."

# 7: Other Versions Of The Hitchhiker's Guide To The Galaxy

## *The Computer Game*

*Story*: The storyline of the *Hitchhiker's Guide* computer game starts out, as in previous versions, with Arthur Dent (the player) waking up to find his house about to be knocked down, then being rescued by Ford Prefect just before the Earth goes the same way. However, later on the story diverges extensively from that of the books, TV series or radio series, with not only old favourites such as Zaphod, Marvin and Trillian but also a host of new characters, situations and ideas.

One notable innovation is that the computer, on occasions, lies to the player, telling him things are in one place when they are in fact somewhere else. Another radical idea is that the player does not necessarily remain as Arthur all the way through the game. Frustrated players who find themselves resorting to violence in an attempt to get information out of Ford Prefect in one scene are alarmed to find that later in the game they have become Ford in that same scene, at which point they have no choice but to suffer the abuse which they previously meted out.

*Background*: With the tremendous popularity of *The Hitchhiker's Guide To The Galaxy* in the 1980s, it was almost inevitable that the concept would be turned into a computer game. However, game graphics of that era were largely limited to crudely-drawn, heavily-pixelated characters with limited animation running around two-dimensional environments, and to follow that route would have been a great disservice to *Hitchhiker's Guide*.

Douglas Adams was a fan of the games produced by a company called Infocom, which were text-only adventures dubbed 'interactive fiction.' The setting, characters and events were all described as in a book, with the player typing instructions to determine (hopefully) the course of events. Other companies also produced text-only adventures, but Infocom were the world leaders, not least because of their state-of-the-art programming which allowed the games to recognise sentence structure and therefore respond more realistically to instructions.

In 1983 Adams approached Infocom (whose biggest hits up till then had been *Zork* and its sequels) with the idea of a *Hitchhiker's Guide To The Galaxy* computer game. He was paired with Steve Meretzky, an Infocom programmer who had not only won awards for his games *Planetfall* and *Sorcerer*, but was also a long-time fan of *Hitchhiker's Guide*. In an early example of e-commerce, the two collaborated by swapping ideas across the Atlantic through modems.

Released on a 5.25 inch floppy disk, *The Hitchhiker's Guide To The Galaxy* was lavishly packaged, with a pair of (cardboard) Joo Janta peril-sensitive sunglasses (as worn by Zaphod Beeblebrox, and designed to prevent the wearer from seeing anything which might alarm them); demolition orders for Arthur Dent's house (in English) and the Earth (in Vogon); a 'Don't Panic' button badge; a microscopic space fleet (effectively an empty polythene sachet); a sales brochure for the *Hitchhiker's Guide*; and a packet of fluff. The game itself offered three different levels of text: 'brief,' 'superbrief' and 'verbose' - the last of which offered as much text as a reasonably-sized novel.

For those players who became completely stumped by the game, an 'invisiclues' hints book could be ordered from Infocom, in which suggestions could be revealed by the use of a special pen.

*Comment*: *The Hitchhiker's Guide To The Galaxy* was a huge hit with both public and critics on both sides of the Atlantic when it was released in late 1984. It was the first time that a major author had been directly involved in the creation of a computer game, and there was extensive adulatory press coverage. Everyone agreed that what Adams and Meretzky had produced was a game unlike any other which, because of its reliance on text, was able to perfectly capture the essence of Adams' work.

As a follow-up, Adams created a totally original game for Infocom called *Bureaucracy*, an epic quest to get a bank to acknowledge a change of address card. This was partly written by Adams' friend Michael Bywater. "Infocom was in the midst of some of the problems which eventually led to their demise at the time," recalled Adams, "and the project kept stopping and starting. Most of the initial work on *Bureaucracy* was mine, but in the end I was less involved with it than I was with the *Hitchhiker's Guide* game."

Both games were released on CD-ROM, together with other titles, in 1994 as *The Lost Treasures Of Infocom Vols. 1* and *2*. A downloadable version of *The Hitchhiker's Guide To The Galaxy* was eventually made available by The Digital Village in conjunction with Comic Relief.

# The Illustrated Hitchhiker's Guide To The Galaxy

Cast: Jonathan Lermit, Tom Finnis, Francis Johnson, Tali, Michael Cule, Janos Kuruz

Hardback: Weidenfeld and Nicolson, 1994

*Story*: The text of *The Illustrated Hitchhiker's Guide To The Galaxy* exactly matches that of the ordinary published novel, with one tiny change. The novel describes Zaphod as having long, blond hair, so a footnote was added to explain why he might appear - to some people - to have short, dark hair.

*Background*: It was in July 1993 that Douglas Adams came up with the concept of *The Illustrated Hitchhiker's Guide To The Galaxy*, using computer-based technology to combine sets, props and actors into fabulous photographic images. To oversee the project - dubbed 'the movie that doesn't move' - Adams suggested Kevin Davies, who had worked on the TV series graphics and the *Making Of The Hitchhiker's Guide To The Galaxy* video.

To generate interest, a test photograph was displayed at the Frankfurt Book Fair. Martin Bower, a veteran of shows such as *Space: 1999*, built a very impressive Vogon constructor ship, incorporating an asteroid on a chain for smashing planets, plus the *Hitchhiker's Guide To The Galaxy* itself and Ford Prefect's electronic thumb.

David Dixon and Simon Jones, the TV series' Ford and Arthur, were approached to pose in the scene, which showed Ford and Arthur standing on the rubble of Arthur's cottage, threatened by a bulldozer, while the Vogon ship roared overhead. However, Jones was unavailable and so Alistair Lock (whom Davies knew from a fan-produced *Doctor Who* spoof, *The Few Doctors*) took his place. This photograph was not used in the book but was published later in *SFX* magazine.

Response at Frankfurt was good, so a full set of images was commissioned. Davies sketched out the scenes which he felt would be most interesting, many of which were extremely peripheral to the plot. A new Ford and Arthur were cast, together with other characters, although no one was needed to play Marvin, a skeletal design which very obviously contained no actor. (This also meant that it could be built at a cost-effective half-size and still appear six feet tall when matted into the pictures.)

All the cast were actors except for Tali, who was a model. Davies himself cameoed as the bulldozer driver; Mike Cule played Mr Prosser; while galactic cops Shooty and Bang Bang were played by Douglas Adams and his agent Ed Victor.

*Comment*: *The Illustrated Hitchhiker's Guide To The Galaxy* is an absolutely gorgeous folly which was the victim of the publisher's uncertainty and a vicious circle of retail. Weidenfeld and Nicolson published a lavish volume with an unusually high price; many potential buyers cooed over it in the shops, and vowed to buy it the moment it was remaindered; because they didn't buy it, it was remaindered, and then they bought it, but by then it was too late.

In retrospect, the publishers would have been better advised to produce a cheaper standard edition and a really OTT drop-dead fabulous collector's edition at a higher price. But retrospect is easy and nobody could have predicted how this unique book would sell.

The designs are simply stunning, far better than anything in the TV series or the comics. There are many surprises and visual jokes hidden away in the backgrounds, including some props from other TV shows to delight hardcore science fiction fans. There is also fun to be had in realising precisely which parts of the text are being alluded to, because in many cases (the Arcturan mega-donkey, the pencil floating across the *Heart Of Gold* bridge) they are far from the obvious ones.

Ironically, time has not been kind to *The Illustrated Hitchhiker's Guide To The Galaxy*. Image manipulation by computer has developed so fast that what caused gasps of incredulity in 1994 is now seen as commonplace. The visual style of the images remains, but the technological thrill of their construction has faded with alarming speed.

Unfortunately, many fans balked at paying £25 (or, in America, $42!) for a novel they already owned, however beautifully produced. Sales were poor, and the book was eventually remaindered. All stocks were acquired by Douglas Adams and signed copies are still available through www.douglasadams.com

## The Comics

*Background*: In 1992 sample artwork was circulated showing Arthur, Ford, Zaphod, Trillian, Marvin and Prostetnic Vogon Jeltz as they were to appear in DC Comics' adaptation of *The Hitchhiker's Guide To The Galaxy*. The three-issue series was a straightforward adaptation of the first novel by John Carnell, with artwork by Steve Leialoha, a British ex-patriot based in Hawaii.

Despite the fact that Douglas Adams had no direct involvement with the comics at all, they still managed to appear in late 1993, exactly one year late.

One year later, Carnell and Leialoha (with inker Shepherd Hendrix) produced a three-part adaptation of *The Restaurant At The End Of The Universe*. A series of 100 *Hitchhiker's Guide To The Galaxy* trading cards was also available at this time, distributed by CARDZ Inc., featuring artwork based on that in the comics. The cards were sold in sealed packs of eight, with randomly inserted 'chase' cards signed by Douglas Adams.

A three-issue comic adaptation of *Life, The Universe And Everything* followed in 1996, once again written by John Carnell, with artwork by Christopher Schenck, Neil Vokes and John Nyberg. Then in 1997 the *Hitchhiker's Guide* comics were collected into a graphic novel, which also included an introduction by Adams and a selection of art from the trading cards. However, the comic-book versions of the second and third novels have yet to receive this treatment.

*Comment*: Many *Hitchhiker's Guide* fans found the comics to be a crushing disappointment. With the feature film stuck in Development Hell, this was an opportunity to present the story in a visual medium, unhampered by effects budgets or interfering Hollywood executives. Yet the published comics completely failed to use that particular medium's potential to reinvent the story, as other versions had done. Instead, they simply retold the novel in a heavily-abridged form through some lacklustre artwork.

*The Hitchhiker's Guide To The Galaxy* comics are a largely forgettable footnote in the *Hitchhiker's Guide* canon, of interest only to completists. Douglas Adams' lack of interest in the medium or involvement in the project is summed up by his response to a query about the comics on his Website a few years later: "I don't know what DC published or didn't publish in the end."

## Don't Panic

Paperback: Titan Books, 1988
Paperback (revised edition): Titan Books, 1993
*Background*: Prior to this one, there has only been one book published about *The Hitchhiker's Guide To The Galaxy*, which is remarkable given the popularity of the series and how many books there are on other cult SF and/or comedy shows. And like the subject it covered, Neil Gaiman's *Don't Panic: The Official Hitchhiker's Guide To The Galaxy Companion* had a long and complex history. It was conceived in 1979 by Stan Nicholls, then manager of London science fiction shop Forbidden Planet and now a successful author in his own right.

"It was intended as Titan's first book," recalls Nicholls. "At that time I was Forbidden Planet's manager, and we organised the first signing Douglas Adams undertook, for the first book, which proved staggeringly successful, with God knows how many copies shifted. As a result of that, FP/

Titan co-owner Nick Landau was receptive to the idea of a companion volume."

Several years later, the project was revived. Neil Gaiman was then a struggling journalist and comics writer who had compiled (with film critic Kim Newman) a book about bad horror and SF. "I did several interviews with Douglas Adams as a young journalist in 1983-84," he said, "or I may have only done one interview and sold it to lots of places - I forget. Anyway, in 1986 Titan Books had the license to do a *Hitchhiker's Guide* companion, but they mislaid the writer they had. Titan asked Kim Newman, who didn't want to do it but suggested me. And I said, 'Sure.' I enjoyed interviewing all the people I needed to talk to and spending time going through Douglas' filing cabinets."

Gaiman spent a year or so ploughing through Adams' files and those of the fan club, ZZ9 Plural Z Alpha, which were maintained by Terry Platt, a fanatical devotee of *Hitchhiker's Guide* with an unparalleled collection of Douglas Adams ephemera.

An American edition of *Don't Panic* was published shortly after the British one and a German translation the following year. When the book was updated in 1993 (one year late!) as *Don't Panic: Douglas Adams And The Hitchhiker's Guide To The Galaxy*, Gaiman was a big name in comics and the new material was written instead by David K Dickson (not to be confused with David Dixon, the TV series' Ford Prefect).

*Comment*: *Don't Panic* (now out of print) was packed with goodies, including unused material from the radio and TV scripts, a partial synopsis of 'Doctor Who And The Krikkitmen', and a facsimile of Douglas Adams' original four-page treatment for *The Hitchhiker's Guide To The Galaxy*. What it didn't have was any pictures. "We had a great set of illustrations for it," lamented Gaiman, "but the publishers decided at the last minute that they weren't going to go with them."

Gaiman's style is light and chatty yet informative and enthusiastic, although occasionally it strays a little too much into faux Douglas Adams. But as the only book ever published about *Hitchhiker's Guide* (until now!), *Don't Panic* is literally essential.

# 8: The Hitchhiker's Guide To The Galaxy Overseas

## *USA*

*The Hitchhiker's Guide To The Galaxy* first appeared across the Atlantic in 1980 as a hardback and was broadcast on National Public Radio shortly after, but few people noticed. Pocket Books changed all this with an advert in *Rolling Stone* in August 1981, offering a free *Hitchhiker's Guide* paperback to the first 3,000 readers to write in, and shortly afterwards Douglas Adams flew to America to discuss with ABC the possibility of remaking the TV series as an American production. However, after a couple of meetings it was discovered that to make the first 22-minute episode to a standard that US audiences would expect would require a budget of $2.2 million. The idea was quickly dropped and never mentioned again.

By the time that Pocket Books published *The Restaurant At The End Of The Universe* in October 1982, Adams' profile was big enough to make the best-seller charts. But it was *Life, The Universe And Everything*, which caused problems. "I think that what happened was that my US publisher was unhappy about using the word 'fuck' because of the number of kids who read the books," explained Adams later. "I was a bit frustrated by that, but then it gave me an idea and I put in the whole Belgium piece."

The problem was the party scene, in Chapter 21 (Chapter 22 in the UK edition), featuring the Rory Award for 'The Most Gratuitous Use Of The Word Fuck In A Serious Screenplay.' Fortunately, in 'Fit The Tenth' Zaphod Beeblebrox had used the swearword 'Belgium' and The Book had explained how it was considered a terrible obscenity in most civilised parts of the galaxy. Douglas added this narration to the chapter and the publishers seemed happy with it.

There are other, less obvious changes: Wowbagger the Infinitely Prolonged, in the opening chapter (British version) tells Arthur Dent, "You're a jerk, a complete asshole," but in the American version 'asshole' has become 'kneebiter' while the word 'shit' later in the book becomes 'swut.' When Ford and Arthur materialise at Lords Cricket Ground, the line, 'In the crowd a man collapsed,' is inexplicably deleted

The Krikkit spaceship, in the British edition, appears with a noise like a hundred thousand people saying "wop" which the Americans changed to "whop," presumably because, despite being used as a purely onomatopoeic term, the word might offend Italians. The chapter numbering in the two editions is also different: the British Chapter 3 is an unnumbered piece between chapters in the US edition, while Chapter 5 is missing altogether, and the Americans split Chapter 22 into three parts.

Interestingly, no such censorship was evident in the American edition of *So Long And Thanks For All The Fish*, which also uses the word 'fuck.' "I think the book was so late they were just relieved to get it!" was Adams' explanation for this inconsistency.

The TV series finally made it to US screens in November 1982, the six episodes re-edited into seven half-hours. Trade journal *Variety* called it, 'an imaginative dud... an interesting comedic idea that didn't get anywhere [with] some clever animated graphics that were indecipherable on a regular-size set.' American videos and a laserdisc release appeared in 1993.

Simon Jones was sent out to America by the BBC to help publicise the series and found the American response very different to the British: "I was ready to say, 'Isn't it impressive? The BBC Special Effects Department working at full blast. Absolute cutting- edge special effects,' and the first thing the disc jockey said to me was, 'Of course, what I liked about it especially was the deliberate tackiness of the effects.' Quick shoe-shuffle, quick rethink, I said, 'Yes, it was of course intentional.'"

The United States have always led the way in publishing omnibus editions of the *Hitchhiker's Guide* novels, starting with *The Hitchhiker's Trilogy* in 1983. This was followed by *The Hitchhiker's Quartet* in 1986 (there was also a boxed set of four paperbacks as *The Universe Of Douglas Adams*). In 1989 'Young Zaphod Plays It Safe' and Douglas Adams' 'Guide To The Guide' were added to the volume which was retitled *The More Than Complete Hitchhiker's Guide To The Galaxy*, followed by *The Ultimate Hitchhiker's Guide To The Galaxy* in 1996, including *Mostly Harmless*. Finally, an omnibus of the five novels without 'Young Zaphod Plays It SaFe' or the 'Guide To The Guide' appeared in 1999 as... *The Hitchhiker's Trilogy*!

There have also been two 'Tenth Anniversary' editions of *Hitchhiker's Guide* books - the first novel and the radio scripts - each of which included a new introduction by Douglas Adams.

## Germany

*Per Anhalter Durch Die Galaxis*, the German edition of *The Hitchhiker's Guide To The Galaxy*, was the first ever translation of one of Adams' works when it was published in 1981. So popular was it that the Germans promptly went ahead and made their own radio series, *Per Anhalter Ins All*, This was adapted from the first six BBC scripts, but each episode in German ran to 50 minutes! The show proved enormously popular and was subsequently released on cassette and CD.

*Per Anhalter Ins All (II)* followed in 1991, a nine-part adaptation of the third and fourth books. Unfortunately, many of the principal cast were unavailable and the resulting series was unpopular with German fans. Much better was a five-part dramatisation of the novel of *Starship Titanic* in 1999.

All of Adams' works have been published in Germany, where *Mostly Harmless* is entitled *Einmal Rupert Und Zuruck* ('once to Rupert and back') and there are two different editions of *Dirk Gently's Holistic Detective Agency*: *Der Elektrische Monch* and *Dirk Gentlys Holistische Detektei*. There are German translations of *Last Chance To See* (book and CD-ROM), *The Deeper Meaning Of Liff*, Neil Gaiman's *Don't Panic* and all three comic-book series. The TV series was dubbed into German in the early 1980s and has been released on video.

In 1994 Douglas Adams visited Germany to give readings which were released on CD as *Douglas Adams Live* but for reasons of international copyright are not available in Britain or America. An even stranger CD, also only released in Germany, is *At The End Of The Universe - Homage A Douglas Adams*. This is an avant-garde jazz suite by Klaus König inspired by the *Hitchhiker's Guide*.

## France

All five *Hitchhiker's Guide* novels and both Dirk Gently adventures have been successfully published in France, and a 12-episode French radio series, a translation of the BBC scripts, was broadcast in 1995.

Uniquely, the French publisher of *Hitchhiker's Guide* also commissioned and published an A-Z encyclopaedia of the books, *Surtout Pas De Panique - Le Guide Du Guide Galactique*, written and compiled by the series' translator, Jean Bonnefoy.

## Finland

For such a small country, Finland has a remarkably active science fiction industry, and also produces a lot of radio drama. Not only have all of Adams' books been published in Finland, but Yleisradio have broadcast far more of his works than the BBC. Terry Pratchett, whose novel *Reaper Man* was adapted for Finnish radio, once commented, "I get the impression that there's only three people in Finnish radio, but they're really great guys with a shitload of money, and they're having the time of their life doing whatever they want to do."

The Finnish *Hitchhiker's Guide* was broadcast in twelve episodes in 1984, adapted from the BBC radio scripts; seven years later, *Life, The Universe And Everything* and *So Long And Thanks For All The Fish* were adapted into a six-episode series featuring the same cast. Finland also enjoyed the only ever professionally dramatised Dirk Gently story, when *The Long Dark Tea-Time Of The Soul* was broadcast in 18 episodes from December 1995.

## *Elsewhere*

*The Hitchhiker's Guide To The Galaxy* has been translated into more than 30 languages, including French, Italian, German, Japanese, Ukrainian, Spanish, Portuguese, Hebrew, Greek, Dutch, Norwegian, Finnish, Hungarian and Polish. Many countries have also published the two Dirk Gently novels and *Last Chance To See*. A few have even published a full translation of Peter Haining's *The Wizards Of Odd* and hence 'Young Zaphod Plays It Safe.'

At least three countries - Germany, Netherlands and Finland - have translated *The (Deeper) Meaning Of Liff*. Though this might sound impossible, in each case the native co-author took care to choose place names which were funny when applied to translations of Adams and Lloyd's definitions, and the results are said to be very good.

In 1995, to celebrate the British hosting of the World Science Fiction Convention, the *Hitchhiker's Guide* Appreciation Society published a small pamphlet collecting numerous versions of Prostetnic Vogon Jeltz's poem, 'Oh Freddled Gruntbuggly,' from foreign editions (and a few specially commissioned translations). It was entitled *A Young Vogon's Garden Of Verse*.

# 9: The Film

The story of the feature-film version of *The Hitchhiker's Guide To The Galaxy* is long, complicated, frustrating and apparently never-ending (unless something startling has happened while this book was at the printer's).

As early as 1979, the idea of a film version was being discussed, with EMI suggested as a possible backer and even George Lucas' name being mentioned in connection with the project. Two years later, after the TV series had been and gone, and with the second TV series definitely cancelled, the idea of a cinema version was raised again. By August 1982, Douglas Adams was telling interviewers, "I think that there is now quite a good chance that there is soon going to be a film."

In December 1982 it was announced that the film rights to *The Hitchhiker's Guide To The Galaxy* had been sold to Columbia Pictures and producer Ivan Reitman, with Douglas Adams contracted to write the screenplay and also acting as associate producer. A few months later, Adams was in Los Angeles, working on a script which was said to combine elements from all three published novels. Concept artist Ron Cobb, who had achieved great acclaim for his work on films such as *Alien* and *Star Trek II: The Wrath Of Khan*, was attached to the project, and Columbia Pictures grandly (and somewhat naively) announced that the film would be released in 1985. Everything looked very promising, and the first draft of the screenplay was handed in to Columbia in September 1983.

First draft screenplays are never filmed, so a second draft was completed in June 1984, by which time Michael White had been added to the project as co-producer. Adams was by now working simultaneously on both the film script and the *Hitchhiker's Guide* computer game. The game appeared in November 1984, just as Columbia was rectifying their schedule, with the film due to commence production in May 1985, for a 1986 release.

Columbia renewed their option in October 1985, at which point Douglas Adams said, "They're still looking for a director. They've got another writer who's still going through my version at the moment, then they're going to give it back to me."

A 'revised draft' was handed in to Columbia in June 1986 with the author credit, 'by Douglas Adams and Abbie Bernstein, based on Douglas Adams' books.' The use of 'and' rather than '&' indicates that Bernstein (a frequent contributor to American SF and horror movie magazines but with no professional movie-writing credits) revised Adams' work rather than collaborating with him. Missing the whole point of *Hitchhiker's Guide* by a mile, and including such unwanted Hollywood-isms as an Arthur-Trillian romance, it was no surprise (and a great relief) that this version did not get made.

By 1987 the project had faltered completely, and Douglas Adams was happy to explain to interviewers where the problem lay. "I didn't want to do a movie version, but eventually ran out of reasons not to," he told them. "[Ivan Reitman and I] had a meeting and he said, 'Douglas, the movie-going public is going to feel jerked off if you tell them that the meaning of life, the universe and everything is 42. We need a big finish.' That's when I knew I was up a gum tree."

To another interviewer, Adams said, "I have written three drafts of the screenplay, each worse than the last, and for the past four years I have often been told that the film is ready to go into production, but they cannot find a director. I was then told that a director had been found and hired, but they were no longer going to make the movie. I view the project as a spectator sport: I may or may not recognise bits when it comes out."

It is clear now that producer Reitman bought the rights to the story without having the slightest clue why it was successful, or in fact understanding it in any way. Comparisons were drawn to the infamous American remake of *Fawlty Towers* which eliminated the 'unsympathetic' character of Basil. Adams succinctly and memorably summed up Reitman as, "The sort of guy who'd buy three gallons of chocolate chip ice cream and then complain about the dark lumps."

Meanwhile, the story emerged that an entirely new creative team was working on the project, headed by no less than David Puttnam. He invited Rocky Morton and Annabel Jankel (creators of the original *Max Headroom* pilot and later directors of *Super Mario Brothers*) to LA to discuss the film, and they in turn discussed the project with Rod Lord, the man behind the TV graphics. But by May 1987, it was announced that this possibility had been abandoned, and the film went into limbo. Simon Jones very adroitly observed, "I'm constantly amused by the progress of *Hitchhiker's Guide* from film company to film company, and figure that we'll all be drawing our pensions before it's actually made into a movie."

Fast forward to June 1992, when Douglas Adams revealed that he was attempting to buy back the film rights to his own book from Columbia. "There are semi-horrendous contractual problems, in that there shouldn't be any contractual problems at all. The fact that there are any contractual problems at all is horrendous," he lamented. At this stage, no less a director than James Cameron was interested in the project.

By October 1993 Adams was confident enough to announce, "It looks as if the movie will now finally be made," and the following February he completed a brand new first draft screenplay, to be shopped around to potential investors. In October 1994, Adams' response to questions about the film was, "It's moved onto the front burner again where it's getting singed to death," to which he intriguingly added, "If the movie doesn't happen I might allow a second television series to go ahead."

The movie's prospects began to brighten in November 1994 when Mike Nesmith - ex-Monkee, inventor of MTV and head of Pacific Arts - was announced as the film's new producer. Things then went quiet again for a few years.

Finally, in January 1998, came the big announcement. *The Hitchhiker's Guide To The Galaxy* would be made into a feature film by Hollywood Pictures. Furthermore, a director was assigned: Jay Roach, who had sprung to prominence with *Austin Powers: International Man Of Mystery* (despite early reports, Roach was not also co-writer).

Since then the project has returned to Development Hell. The release date, initially summer 2000, has been put back further and further, while Jay Roach, who was working on *Austin Powers 2* when the announcement was made, has gone on to make other films. In late 2000, it was announced that the enormous potential cost of the production had caused it to be put 'in turnaround.' In other words, Roach and Adams were both still enthusiastic, but Hollywood Pictures were uncertain and looking to offload the rights to another studio.

Over the years there has been much speculation over casting, all of which is entirely academic since no cast will be assigned until the final draft of the screenplay is approved. In 1996, a list which purported to be Douglas Adams' ideal cast for the six principal characters surfaced, as follows:

Arthur - Simon Jones
Ford - Jeff Goldblum
Slartibartfast - Sean Connery
Zaphod - Michael Keaton
Marvin - Stephen Moore
Trillian - Amanda Donahoe

This list is now out of date. Jones is generally considered too old to play Arthur, although the actor retains the hope that he might land the role of Slartibartfast. Instead, Hugh Laurie is the popular favourite to play the new Arthur Dent. Jim Carrey has been rumoured as a possible Zaphod, although Adams has often said that he would like a black actor in the role, as per *The Illustrated Hitchhiker's Guide To The Galaxy*. Goldblum is a consistently popular choice for Ford Prefect, although when this was mentioned to him in 1996 he had not actually heard of *Hitchhiker's Guide*.

"I find it quite interesting seeing what people's casting ideas are," said Adams recently. "Some of the ideas I see are a bit loopy, but some are interesting because they make me look at actors I wasn't aware of, or because they tell me something about the way people see the characters, which sometimes catches me by surprise."

The one actor whom Douglas Adams has said he definitely does want in the cast is Stephen Moore, whose age is immaterial as he will only be providing the voice of Marvin the Paranoid Android. Marvin himself will be completely computer-generated, as will various aliens and Zaphod's extra head and arm. This is a technique which was not even conceivable when the film was in development at Columbia.

There is no doubt that the saga of the *Hitchhiker's Guide* film will continue for some time yet. The project has now been 'in development' for 22 years; to put this in perspective, it is six years longer than *Star Wars* fans had to wait to see *Episode One*. As it stands, nobody is attached to the project except Douglas Adams (writer), Jay Roach (director) and Roger Birnbaum (producer). Nobody has been cast, and no designs have been made or test footage shot. But the project is far from dead and may yet happen.

In the meantime, any and all newspaper reports that the film is 'just about to be made' are to be treated with extreme caution unless accompanied by an official announcement from Hollywood Pictures.

# 10: Dirk Gently

## *Dirk Gently's Holistic Detective Agency*

Hardback: Heinemann, June 1987

Paperback: Pan Books, October 1988

*Story*: Richard MacDuff discovers, during the course of an incredibly complex adventure, that his tutor at Cambridge, Professor Urban Chronotis, Regius Professor of Chronology, is a time-travelling being. They prevent an evil alien entity from halting the Big Bang and thus causing the universe not to be created. They are assisted in this by an electronic monk, several versions of the Mona Lisa, an eccentric detective name Dirk Gently, and Samuel Taylor Coleridge.

*Background*: In early 1986, eighteen months after the publication of *So Long And Thanks For All The Fish*, came news that Douglas Adams was writing another novel - but it was nothing to do with *The Hitchhiker's Guide To The Galaxy*. It did, nevertheless, have a typically cumbersome Adams title: *Dirk Gently's Holistic Detective Agency*.

The hardback rights to the new book and a sequel were offered around and Douglas signed with Heinemann for £575,000 and with Simon & Shuster (in the USA) for a staggering $2.27 million. And all this before a word had been written. Apparently.

Actually, quite a lot of the words in *Dirk Gently's Holistic Detective Agency* had already been written as Douglas went back to his *Doctor Who* scripts, 'Shada' and 'City Of Death,' reusing elements of the storyline and replacing the Doctor with Dirk Gently.

The book was an immediate best-seller, promoted as 'a detective-ghost-horror-whodunnit-time-travel-romantic-epic.' It was also the first ever desktop-published novel, supplied as camera-ready copy direct from Adams' laser printer. "It was a fascinating and therapeutic way of working," claimed Adams, adding that the technique had shaved five weeks from the production schedule.

*Comment*: Response to Douglas Adams' first non-*Hitchhiker's Guide* novel was, on the whole, quite good. Critics and fans alike generally agreed that it stood up on its own and was certainly comparable to Adams' earlier work. Douglas had proved that it was his name and talent that sold the novels, not the *Hitchhiker's Guide* branding. Quite how many of these fans realised the extent to which *Dirk Gently's Holistic Detective Agency* borrowed from Adams' work for *Doctor Who* is not known - it was certainly unnoticed by the critics.

*Dirk Gently's Holistic Detective Agency* is entertaining, clever, witty and well-structured, but it has one enormous flaw. It is *incredibly* complicated, especially the ending, and few indeed are the people who have understood it after one reading, or even after several. Adams' tendency to allude to things without making them perfectly clear sometimes works (as with Elvis' cameo in *Mostly Harmless*) and sometimes misses completely (as with the original version of 'Young Zaphod Plays It Safe'). The ending of *Dirk Gently's Holistic Detective Agency*, it must be said, is a miss, if not quite a mess.

The complexities of the story are explained on the web in the alt.fan.douglas-adams FAQ (see Chapter 13) and were very skilfully unravelled when the novel was adapted for the stage.

## The Long Dark Tea-Time Of The Soul

Hardback: Heinemann, October 1988
Paperback: Pan Books, October 1989

*Story*: In his second adventure, Dirk Gently gets mixed up with a young lady named Kate Schecter and a range of ancient Norse gods who hang around St Pancras Station. The solution this time lies in something more prosaic than Coleridge's work - a pop record entitled 'Hot Potato' is the key.

*Background*: *The Long Dark Tea-Time Of The Soul* was another bestseller, establishing Dirk Gently as a franchise in its own right. This second outing for the character was actually slightly better than the first, possibly because it was a completely original story. Hopes were high for a third Dirk Gently book, but it has yet to appear.

In 1993, a paperback omnibus edition of both Dirk Gently novels was published, and a hardback omnibus edition appeared in the USA the following year. Professor Chronotis reappeared in a short story in a late 1990s *Doctor Who* annual. The story was uncredited, but was not by Douglas Adams.

*Comment*: Is *The Long Dark Tea-Time Of The Soul* a better book than *Dirk Gently's Holistic Detective Agency*? Opinion is divided. It is certainly better at being a book, in that it was clearly conceived as a novel and wasn't stitched together from parts of used or unused TV scripts. It is also far less confusing than its predecessor and can even be understood on its first reading.

The main problem, which also affected the first book but less so, is that Dirk Gently himself has comparatively little to do. Adams has tremendous fun playing with ideas and characters, twisting them into a plot, and somewhere in there is Dirk Gently. But removing the character of Gently from the book would not harm it to any great extent. That's the curious thing about Dirk Gently: he is a terrific idea and has proved himself, in his limited literary life, to be a popular character with readers. But his influence on his own novels is often minimal.

*The Long Dark Tea-Time Of The Soul* is that rarest of things - a Douglas Adams novel which stands on its own, works on its own, and can be read in isolation from his other works.

## Dirk Gently On Tape

Given that there are only two books in the series, the history of Dirk Gently on audio tape is ridiculously complex.

The first talking book to appear was a two-tape abridged version of *Dirk Gently's Holistic Detective Agency*, read by the author, which was released by Hamlyn Books On Tape in 1988, and shortly afterwards in America by Simon & Shuster Audioworks. The following year, when *The Long Dark Tea-Time Of The Soul* was published in paperback, Simon & Shuster Audioworks released a two-tape abridged reading of that book by Simon Jones. Dove Audio released an unabridged reading, by the author, of *The Long Dark Tea-Time Of The Soul* in 1991, and this was released in the UK in 1992 as part of the BBC Audio Collection, despite the fact that it had never been broadcast! In 1997 Dove finally released an unabridged *Dirk Gently's Holistic Detective Agency*, read by the author but a different recording to the previous abridged version. This surfaced in Britain in 1998 on the Isis label, who had by then released all the Dove *Hitchhiker's Guide* readings. Finally, in late 1999, both unabridged readings were re-released in the United States by Dove as a single eight-tape pack.

Consequently, the two Dirk Gently books have spawned no fewer than eight releases of four readings on five record labels!

## Dirk Gently On Screen

The one and only TV appearance of Dirk Gently was in *The South Bank Show* in January 1992. This was a strangely surreal programme featuring interaction between Douglas Adams' world and his fictional characters. Simon Jones and David Dixon recreated their roles from the TV series, Peter Jones provided some narration, and Marvin put in an appearance (voiced by Stephen Moore), although he had to wear a long overcoat as the BBC could only find his head!

*The South Bank Show* also featured Dirk Gently, played by Michael Bywater, a friend of Adams whose best-known work is probably the Bargepole column in *Punch* and who had worked on the *Bureaucracy* computer game. Two other characters from *Dirk Gently's Holistic Detective Agency*, Richard MacDuff and the Electric Monk, were both played by Paul Shearer.

In 1995 Douglas Adams told an interviewer, "There's a TV series in development at the moment based on Dirk Gently. I can't give you any dates other than to say that at this level of television just the contract took a year to write."

The TV series never progressed beyond an initial idea - using the character but not the plot of either novel. However, a TV movie based on *Dirk Gently's Holistic Detective Agency* was mooted in 1996 and fantasy writer Michael Marshall Smith was brought in to write the script. Smith was ex-Footlights, like Adams, and had been a huge fan of *Hitchhiker's Guide* in his younger days. After a spell writing comedy for TV and radio, Smith turned to fiction and picked up a slew of British and World Fantasy Awards.

"What's going to be the biggest challenge of dramatising Dirk Gently," he mused, shortly after submitting a rough treatment of the script, "is that the character of Dirk is a centre around which things happen. He's not an active character, he sort of pulls in the stuff. It's a writing conceit and that's why it works so well as text. The challenge is going to be dramatising that so that people understand. What I don't want to do is turn it into a rubbish detective thing." However, after a couple of meetings the project was dropped and has not resurfaced since.

Then, in early 2000, Douglas Adams announced that he himself had got as far as page five of a Dirk Gently feature film screenplay. Michael Nesmith, previously attached to the *Hitchhiker's Guide* movie, was named as producer but Adams emphasised that there was no way the Dirk Gently film would happen before the *Hitchhiker's Guide* one.

## *Dirk Gently On Stage*

Like *The Hitchhiker's Guide To The Galaxy*, Dirk Gently has found the theatre stage easier to conquer than the cinema screen. A stage adaptation of the first novel, with its title conveniently shortened to *Dirk*, began life as a school production in 1991. According to the play's Website, "It was very short (about an hour), and by all accounts, amusing but utterly incomprehensible."

In May 1995, a proper stage production of *Dirk* was presented in Oxford by a group of undergraduates. The script was written by Arvind David (who also directed) and James Goss, and the play was produced by Matt Wreford. The show featured excellent costumes and props, professional-quality acting, and innovative computer graphics projected onto a screen above the stage. But what astounded audiences was the script which achieved the almost impossible task of making the plot comprehensible.

The play received glowing reviews and was praised by Douglas Adams, who attended the final performance. "They managed to solve the problem of how you deal with lots of complexities and contradictions by simply ignoring them," he commented. "It was wonderful!"

A revival was staged at the Oxford Playhouse in November 1997, again to great acclaim. David and Goss rewrote the script, even more high-tech computer graphics sequences were included, Wreford returned as producer and the director was Alex Potts. With help from the National Theatre and the National Lottery, the production proved even better than before - people travelled all the way from America just to see it.

## The Salmon Of Doubt

In March 1994, six years after *The Long Dark Tea-Time Of The Soul* was published, Douglas Adams announced that he was working on a third Dirk Gently novel. Initially called *A Spoon Too Short*, the title was swiftly changed to *The Salmon Of Doubt*.

One year later, the book was postponed indefinitely because Adams was too busy with other projects. But a few months further on, the book was back in the works and was scheduled for publication in October 1995. Since that date, *The Salmon Of Doubt* has become a quantum book, phasing in and out of existence.

Douglas Adams said in July 1995, "I'm always nervous about telling people about things I'm working on because anything I say about it almost always turns out to be untrue. With this in mind, the only thing I've told people about the current book, *The Salmon Of Doubt*, is that it's a Dirk Gently book. That now turns out not to be true."

Finding that the book wasn't working properly, Adams eliminated the character of Dirk Gently. However, by then Simon & Shuster had prepared dust jackets proudly displaying the subtitle 'A Dirk Gently Novel'! The book was scheduled for publication in April 1996.

*The Salmon Of Doubt* has remained 'in the works' ever since, with regular claims that it has already been published due to certain Internet bookshops' insistence on listing it, complete with ISBN number. By April 1996, the publication had moved back to October, and in December 1996 the publishers revised that to June 1997. When that date came round, Adams blithely announced that the book had mutated from *Dirk Gently III*, through a completely original work, to *Hitchhiker's Guide Part VI*! "Yes, yet another final one," he admitted. "What has happened is... I've rediscovered the second radio series and realised that there are actually some really good ideas in there, which never got used anywhere else in the *Hitchhiker's Guide* pantheon."

Throughout the whole affair, the only thing that has remained constant is the title, which is completely meaningless. "I chose it to irritate my editor," Adams confessed. "She surprised me by really liking it. In fact, the title is the only thing that has remained in place, simply because it's irrelevant to all different versions of the story."

# 11: Other Work By Douglas Adams

## *Footlights*

Douglas Adams attended St John's College, Cambridge University from 1971-74, and while there was invited to join the legendary Footlights Club. Founded in 1883, Footlights staged an annual comic revue (formally known as the May Week Revue) of songs and sketches and had helped to launch the careers of such comedy giants as Peter Cook, John Cleese, Graham Chapman and the Goodies. Many of the *Hitchhiker's Guide* personnel, including Simon Jones, Mark Wing-Davey, Geoffrey McGivern, John Lloyd, Chris Langham and Joe Melia, were members of Footlights before or during Adams' tenure.

From 1972 onwards, Douglas Adams performed sketches and monologues at numerous 'smoking concerts,' the late-night entertainments staged by Footlights members for their peers which served as try-outs for material for the main revue. Through these 'smokers' he became friends with two other undergraduates, Will Adams (no relation) and Martin Smith (later immortalised in *The Hitchhiker's Guide To The Galaxy* with Ford Prefect's line, "This is Zaphod Beeblebrox from Betelgeuse Five you know, not bloody Martin Smith from Croydon.") As Adams-Smith-Adams, the trio became a major writing force in Footlights, contributing many sketches and often performing them themselves.

Douglas Adams appeared briefly in the 1972 May Week Revue, *Norman Ruins*, not on stage but in a filmed segment. In June 1973, as a reaction against not being chosen to perform in that year's revue, Adams-Smith-Adams staged their own independent revue, *Several Poor Players Strutting And Fretting*, the first of several such productions. By 1974, Adams-Smith-Adams were such a regular fixture in Footlights that they confidently expected to perform in that year's revue, *Chox*, especially as their material accounted for more than half of the script. In the end, however, only Martin Smith was picked for the cast, which also included Griffith Rhys Jones (*sic*), Geoff McGivern and Clive Anderson.

Highlights from *Chox* were broadcast on BBC1 in August and followed by a short-lived Radio 4 series, *Oh No It Isn't!*, produced by Simon Brett; Adams-Smith-Adams were credited as writers on both the TV broadcast and the radio shows.

Douglas Adams, Will Adams and Martin Smith all graduated from Cambridge in 1974, and two years later Douglas was approached by Footlights to direct the 1976 May Week Revue, which reflected the emergence of punk by being entitled *A Kick In The Stalls*. Douglas Adams was also credited in the programme as one of the revue's writers, with Will Adams and Martin Smith providing additional material.

The last ever appearance of Adams-Smith-Adams was a writing credit in a 1981 independent revue, *An Evening Without*, which was a hit on the Edinburgh Festival Fringe of that year. The team of Footlights alumni responsible, calling themselves 'Comic Business,' consisted of Griff Rhys Jones, Martin Bergman, Clive Anderson, Rory McGrath and Jimmy Mulville, and an incredibly rare LP of the show was also produced.

## Monty Python/Graham Chapman

Douglas Adams has always been an enormous fan of Monty Python, and the Python influence on *The Hitchhiker's Guide To The Galaxy* (especially in its early incarnations) is fairly obvious. Through his work with Footlights at Cambridge, Adams was able to meet first John Cleese and later Graham Chapman, with whom he collaborated on various projects.

The fourth and final series of *Monty Python's Flying Circus* was retitled *Monty Python* and was made without John Cleese. Chapman and Cleese had been a writing partnership on the first three series, and consequently Chapman was at a bit of a loose end and seeking other collaborators, one of whom was Douglas Adams.

Adams appears very, very briefly and almost unrecognisably in two *Monty Python* sketches. He is one of the 'pepperpot ladies' in one sketch, and he is a surgeon in another. As he describes it, "You see me for about three frames looking into camera but wearing a surgeon's mask. It's the episode which introduces one character after another after another before getting to the point." He even received a credit for additional material in the last TV episode ever, broadcast in December 1974, and on the album of *Monty Python And The Holy Grail* he receives a credit because part of the linking material between soundtrack clips includes a heavily-revised sketch of his about Marilyn Monroe. This makes Adams one of only two non-members of the team to have contributed comedy material to the Python canon (the other is Neil Innes).

Chapman and Adams also collaborated on a 1977 episode of *Doctor On The Go* entitled 'For Your Own Good' and a one-off sketch show in 1976, *Out Of The Trees*, featuring Simon Jones and Mark Wing-Davey. One sketch from this, 'The Private Life Of Genghis Khan,' was later reworked by Adams into a short story for *The Utterly, Utterly Merry Comic Relief Christmas Book*.

Also of note is *Our Show For Ringo Starr*, an unproduced special for American TV written by Chapman and Adams as a vehicle for the ex-

Beatle. This script was finally published in 1999 in a book called *OJRIL: Old Jokes And Ridiculously Irrelevant Links* and proved to be an uneasy mix of Beatle-esque and Python-esque humour which would have needed a lot of rewrites (and a huge budget) to be broadcastable.

Douglas Adams is also one of several listed co-authors of Chapman's surreal memoir, *A Liar's Autobiography* (published in 1980) although his contribution is very small.

## *Doctor Who*

"I remember when I was at school I wrote an episode of *Doctor Who* just for us to do on the tape recorder," Douglas Adams told an interviewer in 1978. "Daleks being powered by Rice Krispies is about all I remember."

Always a big fan of the long-running series, Adams' first serious attempt at writing for *Doctor Who* was a spec script (i.e. unsolicited) submitted to the show in 1974. This now-lost script was notable only for the idea of the 'B' Ark, a means to rid the world of the useless third of its population who don't actually do anything; this idea was reused in the unmade *Our Show For Ringo Starr*, and finally saw the light of day as the Golgafrinchan 'B' Ark in *The Hitchhiker's Guide To The Galaxy*.

### The Pirate Planet

Broadcast: September 1978

Cast: Tom Baker, Mary Tamm, John Leeson, Bruce Purchase, Andrew Robertson, Bernard Finch, David Sibley, Primi Townsend, David Warwick, Rosalind Lloyd

Director: Darrol Blake

In 1977, while waiting for BBC Radio to decide whether or not they wished to make a series of *Hitchhiker's Guide*, Adams submitted the pilot script for his series to the then script editor of *Doctor Who*, Robert Holmes, as an example of his work. Holmes liked what he saw and commissioned a four-part story from Adams.

Broadcast as part of the six-story 'Key To Time' arc, 'The Pirate Planet' concerned a hollowed-out world which transported itself through space, materialising around other planets and then stealing all their minerals and other material supplies. The cyborg captain of the planet even had an eye-patch and a robotic parrot - this would not be the only time that a character created by Douglas Adams would wander around a TV series with a lifeless plastic thing attached to his shoulder!

To Douglas Adams' enormous surprise, Anthony Read (who had succeeded Holmes) asked him to take over as script editor on the show for the subsequent season (September 1979 to January 1980), during which Adams wrote two scripts.

## City Of Death

Broadcast: September 1979

Cast: Tom Baker, Lalla Ward, Julian Glover, Catherine Schell, David Graham, Tom Chadbon, Kevin Flood

Director: Michael Hayes

In 'City Of Death' an alien steals the Mona Lisa to prevent the explosion that destroyed him. The Doctor must ensure that the explosion actually happened, as it was directly responsible for the existence of life on Earth. John Cleese and Eleanor Bron made a memorable cameo appearance as a couple in an art gallery who mistake the TARDIS for a modern sculpture. This story actually began life as a script by David Fisher, but when it ran into problems, Adams and producer Graham Williams were called in to finish it under the pseudonym 'David Agnew.' Part 4 of this story was, thanks to an ITV strike, the highest-rated episode of *Doctor Who* ever.

## Shada

Not broadcast

Cast: Tom Baker, Lalla Ward, David Brierley, Denis Carey, Christopher Neame, Victoria Burgoyne, Daniel Hill

Director: Pennant Roberts

'Shada' was a chase through space and time which concerned a retired Time Lord posing as a Cambridge Don under the name Professor Chronotis. This story achieved infamy because a BBC technicians' strike prevented its completion, although footage was used in the 1983 adventure 'The Five Doctors' to compensate for Tom Baker's unavailability. It was eventually released on video in 1992, complete with a copy of the script and with Tom Baker bridging the gaps in the footage. Douglas Adams' royalties from the video were donated to Comic Relief.

'The Pirate Planet,' 'City Of Death' and 'Shada' are among the very few *Doctor Who* stories never to have been novelised. There were plans to publish the scripts of 'The Pirate Planet' in 1993, but after being postponed to 1994, the book was cancelled.

Apart from the above, Douglas Adams wrote one other *Doctor Who* story as a film treatment, 'Doctor Who And The Krikkitmen,' which was not only never made but never actually optioned for production. It concerned a race of evil, cricket-playing warrior robots attempting to save their home planet from the time loop to which it had been banished.

This storyline was eventually used for the third *Hitchhiker's Guide* novel, *Life, The Universe And Everything*, with Slartibartfast as the Doctor and Arthur Dent replacing Sarah Jane Smith as the confused Earthling. Although the book claimed to be based on the later episodes of the radio series, it is essentially a novelisation of 'Doctor Who And The Krikkitmen.'

## *The Meaning Of Liff*

Paperback: Pan Books, 1983
Hardback (revised edition): Pan Books, 1990
Paperback (revised edition): Pan Books, 1991

*Background*: *The Meaning of Liff*, co-written by Adams and John Lloyd, is most commonly described as a spoof dictionary. It is a collection of place names, each of which is given an amusing definition. As the introduction puts it: "There are many hundreds of common experiences, feelings, situations and even objects which we all know and recognise, but for which no words exist. On the other hand, the world is littered with thousands of spare words which spend their time doing nothing but loafing about on signposts pointing at places."

The book began life as excerpts from 'The Oxtail English Dictionary' in the 1981 book *Not 1982*, and was subsequently published in its own right as a small, stylish, black paperback. True to the definition of 'Liff' – 'A book, the contents of which are totally belied by its cover. For instance, any book the dust jacket of which bears the words, "This book will change your life."' - the book carried a small orange sticker claiming, 'This book will change your life.'

An American edition of *The Meaning Of Liff* was published in 1984 with some of the more Anglocentric definitions replaced or altered. The idea was revived in 1986 when a handful of additional Liff definitions, by Adams, Lloyd and Stephen Fry, were included in *The Utterly, Utterly Merry Comic Relief Christmas Book*, and an expanded version of the original book, *The Deeper Meaning Of Liff*, followed a few years later. There have even been foreign language versions in Germany, Finland and the Netherlands.

*Comment*: There is no doubt that *The Meaning Of Liff* is one of the oddest entries in Douglas Adams' bibliography. It is also one of the funniest and, because if its bite-size structure, one of the most easily accessible. It is very clear that Adams and Lloyd had tremendous fun with the book, not just in choosing the words and definitions, but in the overall layout. A series of maps becomes progressively sillier and less helpful, the letter K for example being a map of South America with every place name indicated as 'off the map' except the tiny Chilean island of Kent! The equally enjoyable index includes such great entries as 'darkness, groping for objects in,' 'things, various,' 'Wind, Gone With The' and 'bddbbrrddrddrr, things that go.'

## *Last Chance To See*

Hardback: Heinemann, 1990
Paperback: Pan Books, 1991
CD-ROM for Macintosh, 1995
CD-ROM for Windows, 1996

*Background*: In 1986, Douglas Adams was asked by *The Sunday Times* to travel to Madagascar and seek out the aye-aye, a worryingly rare species of lemur. As well as writing his feature for the newspaper's colour supplement, Adams also turned the adventure into a programme for Radio 4.

Realising that he could use his celebrity to highlight his interest in ecology, Adams hatched a plan to repeat and expand the process, travelling around the world with zoologist Mark Carwardine in search of animals threatened with extinction. Originally announced for 1987, the trip eventually happened in 1989 and resulted in the book and radio series *Last Chance To See*.

Response to the book, jointly credited to Adams and Carwardine, was enthusiastic, although as non-fiction it wasn't given as much media coverage as a new Douglas Adams novel would have been. Nevertheless it sold reasonably well and was extensively translated. There was even an abridged audiobook.

"It was a bit rough, I felt," was Adams' view of the radio series, for which he and Carwardine had carried expensive recording equipment around the world. "We were given minimal time for editing and production and the thing was rushed out without a lot of promo. I felt a little aggrieved by the whole thing, to be honest. They only paid Mark and me presenter's fees. Nothing for travel or expenses - we had to pay all of that. We even had to pay the expenses of the producer and the sound recordists. So the radio series left us tens of thousands of pounds out of pocket and without a good program to show for it. I was less than happy."

A second radio series of *Last Chance To See* in 1997 was simply readings, by Adams, from the book.

Computer games aside, Douglas Adams has only ever made one foray into the CD-ROM medium. *Last Chance To See* contained the entire text of the book plus 800 photographs, an unabridged reading of the book by Adams, additional narration recorded especially for the CD-ROM, and an hour of extracts from the radio series.

*Comment*: When asked about his favourite among his own books, Douglas Adams invariably points to *Last Chance To See*, and this is an opinion shared by many of his readers. What seems to have happened is that, after years of writing about bizarre alien creatures on exotic planets, Adams realised that even weirder creatures inhabit the far-flung corners of the Earth, and that somebody should bring them to the human race's attention while they are still here.

The kakapo, for example, is an idea that would have fitted in on any of the extraterrestrial worlds described in (and by) *The Hitchhiker's Guide To The Galaxy*: a flightless parrot whose decline in numbers is blamed by naturalists on the observation that the male kakapo's mating call actually repels the female.

Adams' interest in ecology continues to this day, and he has given frequent talks on the subject. He remains passionately committed to the preservation of endangered species, as evidenced by his enthusiastic support for charities such as the Environmental Investigation Agency, Save The Rhino International and the Dian Fossey Gorilla Fund.

## *Dr Snuggles*

One of the most unlikely credits on Douglas Adams' CV is *Doctor Snuggles*, a Dutch cartoon series about a bumbling but happy inventor who has adventures with his friends while building devices to make the world a better place. Filled with talking trees and happy badgers, it was designed to be the world's first non-violent TV cartoon, and was as twee as animation can get. Adams and John Lloyd wrote two episodes. Peter Ustinov voiced the main character.

"My recollection is pretty dim at this point," admitted Adams, many years later, "but I remember we came up with one episode about a river that was hiding in a cave because someone was stealing chunks of the ocean. I can't remember what the other one was about. It was just a job for a couple of hungry wannabes, but I do recall that we had a lot of fun doing it. I never managed to see the actual programme, so I don't know how they turned out, but I believe that one of them won some awards (which we also never saw, of course...)."

## Other Radio And Television Work

Douglas Adams' precise contribution to the original TV series of *Not The Nine O'Clock News* (produced by John Lloyd) is unclear but he is listed among the contributors to three spin-off books: *Not! The Nine O'Clock News*, *Not 1982* and *Not 1983*. The only element of these books which is very clearly by Adams is a series of definitions from 'The Oxtail English Dictionary' scattered throughout *Not 1982*. Most of these turned up, some slightly amended, in *The Meaning Of Liff*.

On radio, Douglas Adams made occasional contributions to *Week Ending* and *The Burkiss Way*, which in later episodes lampooned *Hitchhiker's Guide* mercilessly. In December 1978, he devised and produced Radio 4's alternative pantomime, *Black Cinderella II Goes East*, which featured a cast drawn entirely from ex-Footlights personnel.

Subsequent forays into radio by Douglas Adams have included the natural history programme *Last Chance To See*, a half-hour tribute to the late Peter Jones, and two short series on new technology.

Apart from *The Hitchhiker's Guide To The Galaxy*, Douglas Adams has only ever created one actual TV programme, which was a one-off, hour-long 1990 BBC production called *Hyperland*. In this dramatised look at information technology, Adams (as himself) falls asleep in front of the television and is guided through his dreams by a 'software agent' played by Tom Baker.

*Hyperland* was broadcast before anybody had heard of the World Wide Web, and in retrospect looks incredibly prophetic, although Adams was wrong as much as he was right. Nevertheless, as probably the last serious attempt to present a popular science view of where communication technology could lead to before it actually got up and went there, the programme is of enormous historical interest.

# 12: h2g2

In 1994, Douglas Adams made a quantum leap from writing scripts and novels when he co-founded The Digital Village (TDV), along with Robbie Stamp and Richard Creasey, both former executives with Central Television. Despite the enormous cumulative business experience of the various TDV board members, it is Douglas Adams as 'Chief Imagineer' who is very much the public face of the company.

Initially, The Digital Village was just a Website, www.tdv.com, which did little more than publicise The Digital Village. All manner of potential projects were mooted, including TV series, books, films, CD-ROMs, Websites and other media not even dreamt of yet.

The first product to appear from The Digital Village was *Starship Titanic*.

## *Starship Titanic – The Game*

*Story*: A giant alien spaceship materialises on Earth – on top of a house, in fact – and the player enters. The ship appears to be deserted apart from a range of increasingly bureaucratic robots, an irritating parrot and a talking bomb. The player must attempt to defuse the bomb while upgrading themself through the ship's various class strata.

*Background*: Starship Titanic was to be Douglas Adams' second great franchise after the success of *The Hitchhiker's Guide To The Galaxy*. The concept actually began life as a throwaway joke in the third *Hitchhiker's Guide* novel, *Life, The Universe And Everything*, referring to a fabulous interstellar liner which underwent Spontaneous Massive Existence Failure. Indeed, the title was briefly considered as being used for another *Hitchhiker's Guide* book.

However, with the establishment of TDV, Adams re-imagined *Starship Titanic* as a combined game and novel franchise, possibly also leading to a movie. The idea was that, rather than a computer game based on a book (as the *Hitchhiker's Guide* game had been in the 1980s) or a novelisation of a computer game, the two would be developed in parallel.

Adams had professed great admiration for the popular adventure game *Myst* and wanted *Starship Titanic* to look equally gorgeous. To this end, he enlisted the help of designers Oscar Chichoni and Isabel Molina, known for their work on the film *Restoration* who between them created a quite stunningly designed spacecraft, with a canal (complete with robotic gondoliers) running the entire length of the ship. A state-of-the-art text parser was also incorporated in order to make conversations with the robots which staffed the ship as realistic as possible.

However, like almost everything else on Douglas Adams' CV, *Starship Titanic* (released in association with Simon & Shuster Interactive) didn't appear on time. The game was officially launched in June 1997 at the E3 computer games conference in Atlanta, and it was hoped to be commercially available later that year, but was put back to January 1998 and finally released in April of that year, thus missing the important Christmas market.

Press build-up had been very positive, with computer magazines cooing over the stunning designs and expectations high for entertainment value because of Adams' involvement (although he was not the sole writer). However, hesitant rescheduling of the launch combined with the non-availability of review copies and technical problems with the few copies that were released in advance severely dented the game's launch.

It did not help that the game was only available for PC, and the Macintosh version, first shown off at the Apple Expo in November 1998, did not appear until March 1999, nearly a year after the PC game. Given Douglas Adams' known preference for Macs, this surprised many people, although he explained that the staggered release was more due to commercial demands than technical ones, and anyway it allowed the Mac version to be more thoroughly tested.

*Comment*: When reviewers finally had the chance to actually play the game, critical response was very mixed. The most frequent complaint was that though the puzzles were wacky and potentially entertaining, many of the solutions were simply arbitrary and could not be arrived at by any means other than constant trial and error. Furthermore the widely scattered elements of the game required a lot of very long and tedious travel around the ship for each attempt.

The characters sadly failed to capture the public's imagination, even the manic parrot which was voiced by Terry Jones. In fact there were two Pythons featured in the game; 'Kim Bread,' the actor playing the talking bomb, was swiftly discovered to be John Cleese. When questioned about this, Adams' straight-faced response was, "I've never heard of this Cleese person you mention."

Although it did win the Software and Information Industry Association's 1998 'Codie' award for 'Best New Adventure/Role Playing Software Game,' the overall response to *Starship Titanic* was disappointing and clearly less than the game's creators were hoping for.

## Starship Titanic – The Novel

Paperback: Pan Books, December 1997

*Story*: The *Starship Titanic* is the most incredible spaceship ever built, but cost-cutting measures mean that immediately after launch it undergoes Spontaneous Massive Existence Failure. It lands on Earth, where three friends board it for no apparent reason and are whisked off into the cosmos.

Classified as the lowest class of traveller, they must overcome a series of obstacles, including upgrading themselves, dealing with the many robots who operate the ship, coping with a manic parrot and defusing a talking bomb.

*Background*: Although it was technically entitled *Douglas Adams' Starship Titanic*, with Terry Jones credited as sole author, Adams and Jones were keen to stress in interviews that this was actually a collaborative work - but a serial, rather than parallel, collaboration. In other words, it was a novel by Jones based on a story by Adams.

With the delays undergone by the game, the novel should have had plenty of time to be written, but for various reasons which cannot be explored here it was actually left until the last moment. Adams and Jones had known each other since the days of the *Monty Python* TV series, and Jones was actually the first name ever rumoured as director of a *Hitchhiker's Guide To The Galaxy* movie. The only previous direct collaboration between the two was the short story 'A Christmas Fairly Story' in *The Utterly, Utterly Merry Comic Relief Christmas Book* which Adams had co-edited in 1986.

Although the American first edition was a hardback, the UK edition was a paperback original. This, combined with minimal point-of-sale material and the delay in the book's release, resulted in the title slipping out almost unnoticed, and it failed to make the book charts. Given the following of the two names on the cover, and that all of Adams' previous books - even *The Meaning Of Liff* - had been best-sellers, this was a major disappointment. A strategy guide to the game was also published and there was a short-lived offer, via the Website, of a collection of items (shower-cap, matchbook, etc.) such as might be found on the starship itself.

*Comment*: Given that this was Jones' first novel, and given the tremendous time constraints, it is no surprise that this book is frankly not very good. Critical response to the novel was lukewarm to say the least, with the general observation being that it read like somebody trying to write in Douglas Adams' style and not quite succeeding.

Even though it managed to be published in time for Christmas 1997, when the game should have been released but wasn't, the book still managed to be a few weeks late, due to difficulties with getting the UK proofs approved while Jones and Adams were touring the USA to sign copies of the American version. The first British edition actually had a terrible formatting problem in the introduction which left several pages with only one or two lines on them.

However, *Starship Titanic* was a genuine success in one part of the world. The German version, *Raumschiff Titanic*, was a big hit as both game and book (on which, it was very noticeable, the writing credit was 'Douglas Adams and Terry Jones'). There was even a German radio serial based on the novel, subsequently released on CD. But outside of Germany, *Starship Titanic* failed to leave the lasting mark on the games market the way its creators had hoped it would.

## h2g2.com

Undaunted, the brains behind TDV prepared for their second venture, h2g2. Since the early days of the company, Adams had talked about producing some sort of Internet search engine, capitalising on the recognition factor of the *Hitchhiker's Guide To The Galaxy* name as a branding tool. What was known until 1998 as 'The Hitchhiker's Guide To The Internet,' was finally launched live on *Tomorrow's World* in April 1999 under the name 'h2g2,' and shortly afterwards the www.tdv.com Website was absorbed into the h2g2.com brand.

h2g2 is described as a 'global Internet community' and has the lofty ambition of effectively recreating for real *The Hitchhiker's Guide To The Galaxy*. Since its launch, a worldwide army of thousands of 'researchers' have contributed information on every subject under the sun, with a team of editors helping to sort and either accept or reject submissions. Though the database thus created continues to grow at an alarming rate, the sheer scale of the project means that it will be some time before it can become the prime repository of knowledge which its creators hope.

Apart from h2g2.com and *Starship Titanic*, TDV's/h2g2's other products have been scanty. Through its Website it sells signed copies of *The Illustrated Hitchhiker's Guide To The Galaxy*, and a video of Douglas Adams reading extracts from the *Hitchhiker's Guide* novels (recorded in Islington in 1995 and previously available in America in both audio and video forms). The company also released an album by guitarist Robbie McIntosh and is credited as production company on Adams' two recent Radio 4 series on information technology, *The Internet: The Last Battleground Of The Twen-*

*tieth Century* and *The Hitchhiker's Guide To The Future With Douglas Adams*.

When Douglas Adams invented the idea of *The Hitchhiker's Guide To The Galaxy*, a hand-held, electronic repository of all knowledge, the idea was science fiction - and satirical science fiction at that. As a story, *The Hitchhiker's Guide To The Galaxy* was never meant to be prophetic in any way. But with the advent of WAP technology making h2g2 available through mobile phones, such a device does now actually exist.

There is something wonderfully ironic in the fact that it has taken less time for technology to turn *The Hitchhiker's Guide To The Galaxy* into reality than for Hollywood to turn it into a film...

# 13: The Hitchhiker's Guide To The Galaxy On The Web

The official site for Douglas Adams, **www.douglasadams.com**, contains some rare writings by Adams, a discussion forum, and a forum to post tributes. How often this site will be updated in the future remains to be seen.

h2g2 is now run by the BBC and can be found at **www.bbc.co.uk/h2g2/ guide**; the original address of **www.h2g2.com** will redirect you to the BBC site. Although h2g2 Ltd is no more, tips for playing *Starship Titanic* can still be found at **www.starshiptitanic.com**, which now redirects you to this rather curious address **http://embark.to/StarshipTitanic**

The BBC has set up a superb site for *Hitchhiker's Guide*, covering not just the TV series but all other incarnations too, at **www.bbc.co.uk/cult/ hitchhikers**. It's packed with information, images, competitions and other stuff - exactly the sort of one-stop *Hitchhiker's Guide* resource which has been sorely needed for so long.

Two other long-running projects in a similar vein to h2g2 are *The Real Hitchhiker's Guide To The Galaxy* (**www.realhhg.org.uk/realhhg.html**) and *Project Galactic Guide* (**www.megadodo.com**). Unlike h2g2, both these sites accept entries on purely fictional topics and are more concerned with humour than information.

*ZZ9 Plural Z Alpha* is the Official *Hitchhiker's Guide To The Galaxy* Fan Club, a fan-run organisation which was founded in 1980. The society publishes a quarterly magazine, *Mostly Harmless* (first published 12 years before the novel of that name!) which is the only up-to-date source for *Hitchhiker's Guide* and Douglas Adams news. A friendly, sociable and on occasions downright silly club, ZZ9 also produces a range of members-only merchandise and holds meetings around the country. The ZZ9 website is at **www.zz9.org**, or you can write for membership information, enclosing an SAE, to: ZZ9 Plural Z Alpha, 4 The Sycamores, Hadfield, Glossop, Derbyshire SK13 2BS, UK.

For those who like such things, there is the newsgroup **alt.fan.douglas-adams**. There are innumerable versions of the alt.fan.douglas-adams FAQ scattered around the web, but they are all hopelessly out of date.

There are many fan-run *Hitchhiker's Guide* sites on the web, mostly run by people who love *Hitchhiker's Guide* but don't have anything useful or informative to say about it. One of the few worth looking at, which is nicely and clearly laid out with some useful bibliographical information and a sparky discussion forum, is **www.floor42.com**.

*Dirk*, the stage adaptation of *Dirk Gently's Holistic Detective Agency*, has an excellent website at **http://dirk.members.beeb.net**.

For any genuine news on the feature film of *Hitchhiker's Guide* (albeit with the occasional ludicrous rumour), the best place to check is **www.corona.bc.ca/films/details/hitchhikersguide.html**.

Douglas Adams was a patron of The Dian Fossey Gorilla Fund (**www.gorillas.org**) and Save The Rhino International (**www.savetherhino.com**), both excellent charities which deserve your support.

Believe it or not, there is an official *Doctor Snuggles* site. It's at **www.doctor-snuggles.com**.

Finally, here are a few unclassifiable oddities: a full list of credits for the Finnish radio adaptation of *The Long Dark Tea Time Of The Soul* is at **www.yle.fi/radioteatern/english/general/soul.htm**; you can see a photograph of Prince Edward enjoying a production of *Hitchhiker's Guide* at **www.bmds.bm/image/1992/hitchhikers%205.jpg**; or why not try the alt.fan.douglasadams FAQ in Hungarian at **http://nostromo.jpte.hu/~dent/guide/faq.html**?

# 14: Douglas Adams - A Select Bibliography

## Books By Douglas Adams

*The Hitchhiker's Guide To The Galaxy* (1979)
*The Restaurant At The End Of The Universe* (1980)
*Life, The Universe And Everything* (1982)
*The Meaning Of Liff* (with John Lloyd, 1983)
*So Long And Thanks For All The Fish* (1984)
*The Hitchhiker's Guide To The Galaxy: The Original Radio Scripts* (1985)
*Dirk Gently's Holistic Detective Agency* (1987)
*The Long Dark Tea-Time Of The Soul* (1988)
*Last Chance To See* (with Mark Carwardine, 1990)
*The Deeper Meaning Of Liff* (with John Lloyd, revised edition, 1990)
*Mostly Harmless* (1992)
*The Illustrated Hitchhiker's Guide To The Galaxy* (1994)
*Douglas Adams' Starship Titanic* (by Terry Jones, 1998)

## Other Douglas Adams Related Books

*A Liar's Autobiography* (by Graham Chapman, with additional material by DA, 1980)
*Not! The Nine O'Clock News* (includes miscellaneous material by DA, 1980)
*Not 1982* (includes miscellaneous material by DA, 1981)
*Not 1983* (includes miscellaneous material by DA, 1982)
*The Utterly, Utterly Merry Comic Relief Christmas Book* (ed. Douglas Adams and Peter Fincham, includes three short stories and miscellaneous other material by DA, 1986)
*The Utterly, Utterly Amusing And Pretty Damn Definitive Comic Relief Revue Book* (includes script by DA, 1989)
*Don't Panic: The Official Hitchhiker's Guide To The Galaxy Companion* (by Neil Gaiman, 1988)
*Hockney's Alphabet* (ed. Stephen Spender, includes chapter by DA, 1991)
*Don't Panic: Douglas Adams And The Hitchhiker's Guide To The Galaxy* (by Neil Gaiman, revised edition, 1993)
*Wordsmiths Of Wonder* (by Stan Nicholls, includes interview with DA, 1993)
*Animal Passions* (ed. Alan Coren, includes chapter by DA, 1994)
*The Great Ape Project: Equality Beyond Humanity* (ed. Paolo Cavalieri and Peter Singer, includes chapter by DA, 1994)

*The Wizards Of Odd* (ed. Peter Haining, includes short story by DA, 1996)

*Douglas Adams' Starship Titanic: The Official Strategy Guide* (by Neil Richards, 1998)

*Monty Python Speaks!* (by David Morgan, includes interview with DA, 1999)

*OJRIL: The Completely Incomplete Graham Chapman* (by Graham Chapman, ed. Jim Yoakum, includes script co-written by DA, 1999)

*Sunset At Blandings* (by PG Wodehouse, includes foreword by DA, 1999)

This select bibliography does not include reprints, omnibuses, audio-books, US editions, translations, CD-ROMs or magazine articles - because if it did, it would take up this whole damn book!

# 15: Afterword To The Second Edition

The first edition of this book was published in April 2001. A copy was sent to Douglas Adams' agent, who forwarded it to Adams' home in Santa Barbara, California later that month.

The book was already slightly out of date, two major events having happened while it was at the printers. The h2g2 site, which had closed down in December 2000, re-emerged as an adjunct to the BBC website, and a new graphic adventure game of *Hitchhiker's Guide* was unveiled. Developments of this sort were only to be expected.

On 11th May 2001, while exercising in his local gym, Douglas Adams suffered a massive, fatal heart attack. No one expected that.

The news rapidly spread around the globe, with major obituaries and tributes published in every important newspaper, magazine and website. A funeral was held in California a few days later, and a memorial service in London in September.

A documentary/tribute programme was immediately commissioned by the BBC. *Douglas Adams: The Man Who Blew Up The Earth*, broadcast in August 2001, featured contributions from friends and colleagues, as well as rarely seen archive footage. Later that month, a 'Douglas Adams Day' was staged at the National Film Theatre, and Radio 4 ran a tribute programme in early September.

A collection of rare or unpublished material was announced for publication in late 2001. This was expected to include the most recent draft of the *Hitchhiker's Guide* feature film screenplay, together with whatever existed of *The Salmon Of Doubt*. New editions of the *Hitchhiker's Guide* novels, with jackets designed by Pink Floyd album cover artist Storm Thorgersson, were already planned for publication in Spring 2002, and were brought forward to tie in with the new book. The DVD release of the TV series was also fast-tracked for release in November, including the complete Making Of documentary and many other interesting items.

Douglas Adams' sudden passing was a terrible shock to his family, friends and fans, and a great loss to the world. The subsequent outpouring of emotion showed the high esteem in which he was held, not only as a comic novelist but also as a technological guru and an ecological advocate. He was admired, he was loved, and he leaves a very tall hole in the universe.

So long, Douglas, and thanks...

# The Essential Library

Currently Available

Film Directors:

Woody Allen (£3.99)
Jane Campion (£2.99)
Jackie Chan (£2.99)
David Cronenberg (£3.99)
Alfred Hitchcock (£3.99)
Stanley Kubrick (£2.99)
David Lynch (£3.99)
Sam Peckinpah (£2.99)
Orson Welles (£2.99)
Steven Spielberg (£3.99)

Tim Burton (£3.99)
John Carpenter (£3.99)
Joel & Ethan Coen (£3.99)
Terry Gilliam (£2.99)
Krzysztof Kieslowski (£2.99)
Sergio Leone (£3.99)
Brian De Palma (£2.99)
Ridley Scott (£3.99)
Billy Wilder (£3.99)
Mike Hodges (£3.99)

Film Genres:

Film Noir (£3.99)
Horror Films (£3.99)
Spaghetti Westerns (£3.99)
Blaxploitation Films (£3.99)

Hong Kong Heroic Bloodshed (£2.99)
Slasher Movies (£3.99)
Vampire Films (£2.99)

Film Subjects:

Laurel & Hardy (£3.99)
Steve McQueen (£2.99)
The Oscars® (£3.99)
Bruce Lee (£3.99)
Bollywood (£3.99)

Marx Brothers (£3.99)
Marilyn Monroe (£3.99)
Filming On A Microbudget (£3.99)
Film Music (£3.99)
French New Wave (£3.99)

TV:

Doctor Who (£3.99)

Literature:

Cyberpunk (£3.99)
Hitchhiker's Guide (£3.99)
Terry Pratchett (£3.99)
Agatha Christie (£3.99)

Philip K Dick (£3.99)
Noir Fiction (£2.99)
Sherlock Holmes (£3.99)

Ideas:

Conspiracy Theories (£3.99)
Feminism (£3.99)

Nietzsche (£3.99)

History:

Alchemy & Alchemists (£3.99)
American Civl War (£3.99)

The Crusades (£3.99)
American Indian Wars (£3.99)

Available at all good bookstores, or send a cheque to: **Pocket Essentials (Dept HHG2), 18 Coleswood Rd, Harpenden, Herts, AL5 1EQ, UK**. Please make cheques payable to 'Oldcastle Books.' Add 50p postage & packing for each book in the UK and £1 elsewhere.

US customers can send $6.95 plus $1.95 postage & packing for each book to: **Trafalgar Square Publishing, PO Box 257, Howe Hill Road, North Pomfret, Vermont 05053, USA**. e-mail: tsquare@sover.net

Customers worldwide can order online at **www.pocketessentials.com**.